Unveiling Semiotic Codes of Fake News
and Misinformation

Tatiana Iskanderova

Unveiling Semiotic Codes of Fake News and Misinformation

Contemporary Theories and Practices for Media
Professionals

Tatiana Iskanderova
Prague, Czech Republic

ISBN 978-3-031-53750-9   ISBN 978-3-031-53751-6   (eBook)
https://doi.org/10.1007/978-3-031-53751-6

Cover illustration: © Melisa Hasan

This Palgrave Macmillan imprint is published by the registered company Springer Nature
Switzerland AG
The registered company address is: Gewerbestrasse 11, 6330 Cham, Switzerland

Paper in this product is recyclable.

CONTENTS

ABBREVIATIONS

B	Being
NB	Not-Being
NS	Not-Seeming
S	Seeming

LIST OF FIGURES

CHAPTER 1

Introduction

Abstract This chapter seeks to present the extensive exploration titled *Unveiling Semiotic Codes of Fake News and Misinformation*. Embracing a distinctive perspective, it centers on scrutinizing dyadic and triadic semiotic frameworks—recognized as fundamental elements crucial for acquiring a nuanced comprehension of the intricate nature of fake news and misinformation. The chapter concludes by outlining a roadmap for the entire book. Each subsequent chapter is briefly delineated, providing insight into the thematic content and structural organization of the overarching exploration. This aids in guiding readers through forthcoming discussions and analyses, establishing a cohesive framework to understand the broader implications of semiotic codes in the context of misinformation.

Keywords Semiotics · Fake news · Misinformation · Media · Narratives

About the Book

In contemporary communication, the challenge of effectively conveying information while ensuring its resonance with the audience, relevance, and engagement poses a significant dilemma for communicators. Semiotics, with its focus on message content and the reception process, emerges as an invaluable framework and toolkit for creating communication content across diverse genres.

This exploration, titled *Unveiling Semiotic Codes of Fake News and Misinformation*, takes a rigorous approach to examining the construction and dissemination of deceptive narratives across various media channels. By delving into the intricate web of symbols, signs, and meanings, the publication seeks to unravel the underlying semiotic codes employed in the generation of fake news and misinformation.

Employing a distinctive standpoint, the publication investigates both dyadic and triadic semiotic perspectives as foundational elements for understanding the complexities inherent in fake news and misinformation. The dyadic perspective considers the relationship between two elements, such as the signifier and the signified, shedding light on the nuanced ways in which deceptive narratives manipulate meanings. Simultaneously, the triadic perspective explores the dynamic interplay of three components, offering a comprehensive understanding of how symbols, their interpretations, and their impacts contribute to the deceptive nature of information.

By elucidating these semiotic perspectives, the book not only aims to unveil the mechanics behind the creation and dissemination of deceptive narratives but also seeks to contribute significantly to the scholarly discourse on the intricacies of communication in the context of misinformation. The multifaceted exploration aligns with a broader commitment to fostering critical thinking and media literacy, providing readers with valuable insights into the semiotic dimensions of contemporary information challenges.

Book Structure

As mentioned previously, this book presents fresh perspectives on the construction and transmission of critical issues through various media channels, with a specific focus on the dyadic and triadic semiotic perspectives. Through in-depth analyses of language, images, and symbols employed in media production, the book unveils the strategic use of these elements to create and reinforce false narratives, manipulating common beliefs.

In Chapter 2, the book elucidates the essence of semiotics, providing readers with a comprehensive understanding of the study of signs and symbols. This foundational chapter sets the stage for a deeper dive into semiotic analyses. Readers are guided through the intricate world of semiotics, gaining insights into the ways in which signs and symbols convey meaning, laying a robust groundwork for the subsequent exploration.

Chapter 3 delves into the core of semiotic theories, exploring both dyadic and triadic models of signs. It lays the foundation for decoding the semiotic nuances of fake news, drawing on Ferdinand de Saussure's dyadic model, Roland Barthes's nuanced semiotic theory, and Algirdas Julien Greimas and Joseph Courtés' veridictory square. The synthesis of these theories contributes to a rich tapestry of understanding, allowing readers to grasp the multifaceted nature of semiotics in the context of deceptive narratives.

Moving on to Chapter 4, the book reveals the heart of its exploration as semiotic theories are applied to real-world instances of fake news, offering tangible insights. From Roland Barthes's analysis of deepfakes in an Indian election campaign to the examination of Charles William Morris's semiotic dimensions in the context of fabricated narratives, each section provides a nuanced understanding of the semiotic codes at play. The analysis goes beyond theoretical frameworks, bridging the gap between academic discourse and practical applications.

Supplementing the theoretical discourse, Chapter 5 provides practical exercises offering readers a hands-on approach to recognizing and deconstructing deceptive narratives. Ranging from the application of Roland Barthes's semiotic theory to Charles William Morris's syntactic, semantic, and pragmatic analysis, these exercises enhance readers' ability to engage with the subject matter. By actively participating in these exercises, readers develop practical skills that empower them to critically evaluate and interpret the semiotic dimensions of information.

Drawing on detailed case studies, the author provides valuable insights into recognizing and deconstructing fake news and misinformation. This timely and crucial book is a must-read for academics, researchers, journalists, policymakers, influencers, and anyone concerned with the impact of fake news, misinformation, and semiotic codes on public opinion. It not only equips readers with theoretical knowledge but also empowers them with practical tools to navigate the intricate landscape of contemporary media challenges.

CHAPTER 2

What Is Semiotics?

Abstract This chapter explores the field of semiotics and its impact on decoding signs in media. It introduces the concept of signs, emphasizing their role in unraveling meanings, ideologies, and cultural references. The chapter examines dyadic and triadic semiotics, shedding light on how signs, from visual elements to language, convey nuanced meanings. Through insightful discussions on the applications of semiotics, particularly in advertising, the chapter accentuates the persuasive potency of signs in shaping contemporary societal perceptions. In conclusion, it underscores the ongoing relevance of semiotics across linguistics, media studies, marketing, and cultural analysis, emphasizing its pivotal role in decoding the intricate language of symbols in our daily interactions and understanding of the world.

Keywords Sign · Dyadic semiotics · Triadic semiotics · Media communication · Contemporary societal perceptions

INTRODUCTION: SEMIOTICS AND MEDIA

Semiotics, as a captivating field of study, investigates the multifaceted realm of signs and symbols, shedding light on the intricate ways meaning is constructed across various modes of communication (Chandler, 1994).

© The Author(s), under exclusive license to Springer Nature   5
Switzerland AG 2024
T. Iskanderova, *Unveiling Semiotic Codes of Fake News and Misinformation*, https://doi.org/10.1007/978-3-031-53751-6_2

Within the expansive scope of semiotics, the exploration of signs extends beyond mere symbols to encompass a rich tapestry of linguistic, visual, and cultural elements. In the context of media content, semiotics assumes a pivotal role in unraveling the layers of meaning embedded within visual and auditory elements. This interdisciplinary approach allows us to comprehend the intricate interplay of signs, offering a nuanced understanding of how meaning is constructed and conveyed through diverse communicative modalities.

When applied to the realm of media content, semiotics serves as a powerful tool for decoding the intricate semiotic codes employed by media creators. Signs in media can manifest in various forms, including images, symbols, language, and even the arrangement of elements within a frame or scene. The visual symbols and metaphors, the linguistic choices made in narration or dialogue, and the spatial organization of elements all contribute to the semiotic landscape of media.

By delving into the semiotic dimensions of media, we gain the ability to decipher the hidden meanings, ideologies, and cultural references that media creators seek to convey. Images within advertisements, for instance, go beyond the surface to communicate values, aspirations, and societal norms. The choice of language in news reporting carries with it layers of bias, framing, and perspective. Understanding these signs allows us to navigate the complex web of meanings that permeate media messages, making us more discerning consumers of information.

The study of semiotics in media goes beyond the surface interpretation of visual and auditory stimuli. It involves a deep exploration of how signs operate within specific cultural contexts, influencing and reflecting societal values. Semiotics becomes a key to unlocking the cultural codes embedded in media, revealing the subtle ways in which meaning is negotiated, contested, and constructed.

In essence, semiotics equips us with the analytical tools to engage critically with media content, fostering a more profound appreciation for the complexities of communication. By deciphering the semiotic codes present in various forms of media, we gain insights into the intentional and sometimes subtle ways in which messages are crafted, contributing to our broader cultural understanding.

For instance, in advertising, semiotics plays a pivotal role in dissecting how symbols and images are strategically employed to evoke specific emotions or associations in the audience. Consider a perfume advertisement: the use of a rose as a symbol conveys not only the fragrance but also notions of romance and elegance, appealing to a desired emotional response.

Likewise, in cinema, the arrangement of shots, choice of colors, and even the soundtrack all function as signs contributing to the film's overall meaning. In a suspenseful scene, the combination of low lighting, tense music, and rapid editing creates a sense of unease, effectively conveying the filmmaker's intended mood and heightening the audience's emotional engagement.

By exploring the role of semiotics in media content, we gain a deeper appreciation for the intentional and often subtle ways in which creators communicate messages, influence perceptions, and contribute to the cultural discourse.

Concept of Sign

At the core of semiotics is the concept of a sign, considered the basic unit of analysis in this field. In this context, a sign can be defined as any element that conveys meaning, encompassing words, images, sounds, gestures, and more. It serves as the foundational communication element, symbolizing or representing something beyond its immediate, material existence.

A sign is essentially a representation, a link between the material and the abstract, the visible and the conceptual. What gives a sign its significance is the relationship between the sign itself and what it signifies. This relationship can take one of two forms: arbitrary or conventional. In an arbitrary relationship, there is no intrinsic or inherent connection between the sign and its meaning. An exemplary case is that of traffic signals. The color red signifies "stop," yet there is no inherent connection between the color red and the action of halting. The association arises from societal consensus and agreement.

Conversely, a conventional relationship is rooted in cultural or social norms and conventions. In this context, the connection between the sign and its meaning is established through shared understandings within a specific community or culture. For example, the word "apple" represents a specific type of fruit, and its meaning is universally understood due to language and cultural conventions.

Semiotics acknowledges that signs are not static entities; they possess dynamic and complex capabilities in communicating and shaping social and cultural practices. Advertising, for instance, is a prominent application of semiotics. Advertisers adeptly use signs to influence consumer behavior by creating specific images and impressions associated with their products or services. They skillfully manipulate semiotic elements to connect with their target audience's desires and values, thus illustrating the dynamic and persuasive power of signs in contemporary society.

DYADIC AND TRIADIC SEMIOTICS

Now, let's examine the structure of signs. Dyadic semiotics, a perspective within semiotics, dissects a sign into two fundamental components: the signifier and the signified. The signifier constitutes the physical or sensory aspect of the sign, be it a sound, an image, or a word (de Saussure, 1959). The signified, on the other hand, represents the conceptual or abstract meaning that the signifier points to. For instance, when we encounter the word "apple," the signifier is the written or spoken word itself, and the signified is the mental image and understanding of the fruit (Chandler, 1994).

Triadic semiotics, on the other hand, presents a more intricate view of signs by introducing the concept of an *interpretant*. In this perspective, a sign is perceived as having three components: a *sign-object*, a *sign vehicle*, and an *interpretant*. The *sign-object* is the entity or concept that the sign refers to. The *sign vehicle* is the physical or sensory element of the sign, whether it is a word or an image. The *interpretant* is a crucial element, representing the meaning that emerges from the interaction between the sign-object and the sign vehicle (Peirce, 1958). In this way, triadic semiotics offers a nuanced perspective on how signs convey meaning, considering not only the elements themselves but also the interpretive processes that occur (Chandler, 1994).

Both dyadic and triadic semiotic perspectives are invaluable in unveiling the complex nature of signs and their role in conveying meaning and transmitting messages across various forms of media. Understanding the dynamics of signs enriches our comprehension of communication and empowers us to decode the language of symbols that envelop us in our everyday lives.

The realm of semiotics continues to be a vibrant and evolving field of study, with applications in diverse domains such as linguistics, media studies, marketing, and cultural analysis. The recognition of the complex interplay between signs and their meanings underscores the importance of semiotics in understanding how we make sense of the world and communicate within it.

REFERENCES

Chandler, D. (1994). *Semiotics for beginners.* http://visual-memory.co.uk/daniel/Documents/S4B/sem01.html

de Saussure, F. (1959). *Course in general linguistics* (C. Bally & A. Sechehaye, Eds., W. Baskin, Trans.). The Philosophical Library.

Peirce, C. S. (1958). *The collected papers of Charles Sanders Peirce* (Vols. 1–8, A. W. Burks, Ed.). Harvard University Press.

CHAPTER 3

Two Major Theories of Sign (Dyadic and Triadic) and Their Application to Fake News Analyses

Abstract This chapter builds upon the foundational concepts established in the preceding section, to elucidate the core theories that govern the study of signs—specifically, the dyadic and triadic perspectives. As the intellectual landscape is navigated, the primary objective is to clarify these perspectives, equipping readers with essential tools for a more profound understanding of the application of semiotics in the analysis of fake news. Throughout this chapter, insights from semiotic luminaries such as Ferdinand de Saussure, Roland Barthes, Algirdas Julien Greimas, Joseph Courtés, Charles Saunders Peirce, and Charles William Morris are drawn upon. Their contributions provide valuable perspectives on how signs shape our understanding of the world, laying the groundwork for a more profound analysis of deceptive narratives within the context of fake news.

Keywords Sign · Fake news · Core semiotics theories · Triadic perspective · Dyadic perspective

© The Author(s), under exclusive license to Springer Nature Switzerland AG 2024
T. Iskanderova, *Unveiling Semiotic Codes of Fake News and Misinformation*, https://doi.org/10.1007/978-3-031-53751-6_3

INTRODUCTION

This chapter serves as a direct continuation, building upon the groundwork laid in the previous section. As we traverse the intellectual landscape, our primary objective is to illuminate the core theories that govern the study of signs—the dyadic and triadic perspectives. By elucidating these perspectives, we equip readers with essential tools for a more profound exploration into the application of semiotics to the analysis of fake news.

It begins by revisiting the essence of semiotics, reinforcing key concepts that form the backbone of this field. Through a careful examination of dyadic and triadic theories, we aim to demystify the intricacies of how signs operate in human communication. This theoretical foundation is not only a precursor to a more nuanced understanding of semiotics but also a crucial stepping stone toward a practical exploration of its real-world applications.

Throughout this chapter, we will draw upon the wisdom of semiotic luminaries such as Ferdinand de Saussure, Roland Barthes, Algirdas Julien Greimas, Joseph Courtés, Charles Saunders Peirce, and Charles William Morris. Their contributions provide valuable insights into how signs shape our understanding of the world, setting the stage for a more profound analysis of deceptive narratives in the context of fake news.

The theoretical groundwork laid in the preceding chapter serves as a guiding beacon, directing our attention to the practical application of semiotics in unraveling the complexities of fake news. Our exploration is not confined to the theoretical realm but extends into the practical domain, where the theoretical underpinnings of semiotics meet the challenges posed by deceptive narratives.

DYADIC MODEL OF THE SIGN

Ferdinand de Saussure's Dyadic Model of the Sign

As mentioned in the preceding chapter, semiotics is primarily concerned with the study of signs and their associations with both objects and meanings. Two prominent contemporary models define what constitutes a sign: dyadic and triadic.

This section is dedicated to exploring Saussure's theory of the sign. Saussure's model of the sign follows the dyadic tradition (see Fig. 3.1).

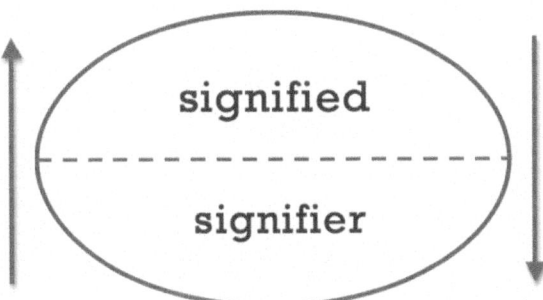

Fig. 3.1 Ferdinand de Saussure's model of the sign: signified and signifier

Focusing predominantly on linguistic signs, such as words, Saussure characterizes a sign as comprising two fundamental components, the *signifier* and the *signified* (de Saussure, 1959, p. 66).

In this model, the sign constitutes the entirety that emerges from the fusion of the signifie*r* with the signified. The connection between the signifier and the signified is denoted as *signification*, and in Saussure's diagram, this concept is visually represented through arrows. The horizontal broken line that separates these two vital components of the sign is commonly referred to as "the bar," as illustrated in Fig. 3.1.

The signifier can take various forms, whether it's a spoken or written word, an image, or even a sound that represents something in the world, such as a "tree." The signified, on the other hand, is the mental concept or idea of that thing; in this case, the concept of a tree. The sign, then, serves as the bridge that unites the signifier and the signified into a cohesive and meaningful unit, as depicted in Fig. 3.2. Stated differently, the sign is the relationship between the concept and the representation of that concept (de Saussure, 1959, p. 67).

Saussure's insights into the nature of signs and the intricacies of the relationship between the concept and its representation have profoundly influenced the field of semiotics and our understanding of language and communication. These concepts continue to shape how we perceive and analyze signs and their roles in our everyday lives.

For example, when reminiscing about my childhood, a vivid memory surfaces: the stuffed purple rabbit that was my cherished companion. This purple rabbit, in the realm of semiotics, was the signifier—a tangible representation of something deeper. Consider what a stuffed animal could

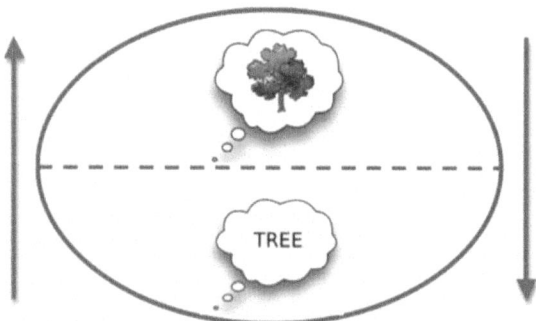

Fig. 3.2   Ferdinand de Saussure's model of the sign: image and concept

signify to a child. In my case, that purple rabbit held profound significance; it signified safety, warmth, and comfort. Whenever I entered my room and gazed upon my stuffed purple rabbit, it was a reassuring sign that everything was okay in my world.

However, as time flows steadily forward, that once-beloved stuffed purple rabbit has transformed into a poignant memory. I can't even recall its name now, a detail that was once so crucial to me. Instead, this rabbit has evolved into a sign of something else entirely. It remains a signifier, but what it signifies has shifted. It now symbolizes my early childhood when the world felt calm, secure, and inviting. The rabbit, in its current form, stands as a sign of my youthful innocence, my hard-to-remember past, much like the name of that cherished toy.

In Ferdinand de Saussure's pioneering semiotic framework, a linguistic sign isn't merely a connection between an object and a name. Instead, it bridges a concept (the signified) and the "sound pattern" (the signifier). It's essential to recognize that this "sound pattern" doesn't represent an actual sound; it is the mental impression of a sound, as perceived by an individual's senses. In essence, both the signifier (the "sound pattern") and the signified (the concept) are fundamentally psychological (de Saussure, 1959, p. 67). They exist in the realm of the mind, not in the physical world as tangible substances.

In contemporary interpretations of Saussure's model, the essence remains, but it has taken on a more materialistic perspective. The signifier is now frequently understood as the material or physical form of the sign—something that can be seen, heard, touched, smelled, or tasted.

This shift in perspective acknowledges the concrete, sensory aspects of the signifier, moving away from the purely psychological understanding proposed by Saussure.

This evolution in the understanding of signs and signifiers demonstrates the dynamic nature of semiotics. It adapts to our evolving comprehension of the world and how we engage with it. The stuffed purple rabbit, once a source of comfort and security, now symbolizes not just my childhood but the ever-changing nature of how we interpret the world through the lens of signs and symbols.

To illustrate the concept of signs further, consider a linguistic example. When we encounter the word "open" on a shop doorway, it serves as a sign composed of two key components (Chandler, 1994):

1. The signifier: In this case, it's the written word "open."
2. The signified concept: This represents the idea that the shop is currently open for business.

For a sign to exist, it must possess both a signifier and a signified. You can't have a signifier that is entirely devoid of meaning or a signified concept that lacks any definable form. A sign is essentially a recognizable combination of a specific signifier with a particular signified. What's fascinating is that the same signifier, like the word "open," can take on a different signified, thus becoming a distinct sign. For instance, if the word "open" is mentioned next to a push-button inside an elevator, it signifies the action of "pushing to open the door."

Moreover, many different signifiers could represent the concept of "open." For instance, on top of a packing carton, a small outline of a box within an open flap can signify "open this end." Each unique pairing of a signifier and signified constitutes a different sign, showcasing the versatility of this concept.

Saussure points out that sound and thought (or the signifier and the signified) are as inseparable as the two sides of a piece of paper. They are "intimately linked" in the mind by an associative link—each triggers the other. Saussure presented these elements as entirely interdependent, with neither existing independently of the other. In the context of spoken language, a sign cannot consist solely of sound without sense or sense without sound (de Saussure, 1959, pp. 114–115). The two arrows in the diagram symbolize their dynamic interaction (see Fig. 3.3).

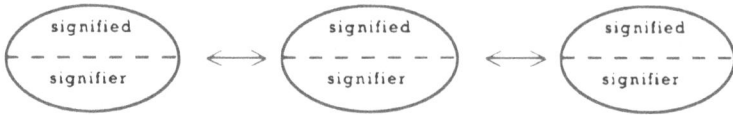

Fig. 3.3 Ferdinand de Saussure's model of the sign within the context of spoken language

For Saussure, signs primarily refer to each other within the language system. In his view, "everything depends on relations" (de Saussure, 1959, p. 115). No sign exists in isolation; it gains meaning and significance only in relation to other signs, as depicted in Fig. 3.3. Both the signifier and the signified are fundamentally relational entities. This notion can be challenging to understand, as we might feel that an individual word such as "tree" does have some meaning for us on its own. However, Saussure's argument is that the meaning of "tree," for example, depends on its relation to other words within the linguistic system, such as "bush."

This profound perspective on signs and their interdependence has significantly influenced the study of language and communication, shedding light on how meaning is constructed and conveyed within linguistic and semiotic systems.

Roland Barthes's Semiotic Theory

Roland Barthes's Theory of Denotation, Connotation and Myth
Barthes' approach often positions him as a structuralist, closely aligning with the foundational principles of Saussure's semiotics. However, his work sometimes displays poststructuralist undertones, adding complexity to the theoretical framework. In this section, we explore Barthes's theory, with a particular emphasis on the ideas of *denotation, connotation*, and *myth*, providing insights into their importance for comprehending the complexities of semiotics.

Saussure's model of the sign plays a pivotal role in Barthes' thinking. As discussed in the preceding section, this model hinges on the distinction between the signifier and the signified. The signifier, in essence, is the visual or linguistic representation used to symbolize something else, while the signified stands for what that representation encapsulates—be it a concrete entity, a concept, or an emotional response. Saussure's insight highlights the inseparable nature of sound and thought, the signifier, and the signified. He viewed them as intricately linked in the mind through an associative connection, with each aspect triggering the other, forming a symbiotic relationship.

Roland Barthes astutely observed that Saussure's model predominantly emphasizes denotation while overlooking the significance of connotation. Subsequent theorists, particularly Barthes himself, undertook the task of exploring this important dimension of meaning. According to his theory, the signified can sometimes exist independently of language and social constructs, whereas the signifier is intrinsically bound to these constructs. Furthermore, the relationship between the signifier and the signified is fundamentally arbitrary. This means that there is no inherent reason why a specific signifier is used to represent a particular signified. Language and culture dictate these connections, and there are multiple ways to express a single signified, each being equally valid.

What do the above-mentioned denotation and connotation mean in the context of Barthes' semiotic theory?

Denotation, often described as the definitional, literal, or common-sense meaning of a sign, refers to the straightforward interpretation that a sign offers (Chandler, 1994). When dealing with linguistic signs, the denotative meaning aligns with what you would find in a dictionary's definition. For instance, in the case of a characteristic blueberry color, the denotation of the word "blue" is the blue color of the fruit.

Connotation, on the other hand, introduces a layer of complexity and depth to the sign. It encompasses the socio-cultural and personal associations and implications of the sign. Connotations are intrinsically tied to the interpreter's characteristics such as their class, age, gender, ethnicity, and so on. It's in the realm of connotation that signs become poly-semic, capable of bearing multiple, interconnected meanings. Denotation is often likened to a digital code—precise and straightforward—while connotation resembles an analog code, rich with nuanced interpretations and cultural resonances.

Barthes's theory of the sign reveals that there exist different orders of signification. The first order of signification is denotation, where a sign consists of a signifier and a signified, forming a straightforward connection between a word and its immediate, literal meaning. Connotation is a second order of signification, which uses the denotative sign as its signifier and attaches to it an additional signification. In this framework, connotation essentially becomes a sign that is derived from the signifier of a denotative sign, thereby creating a chain of connotations (Barthes,

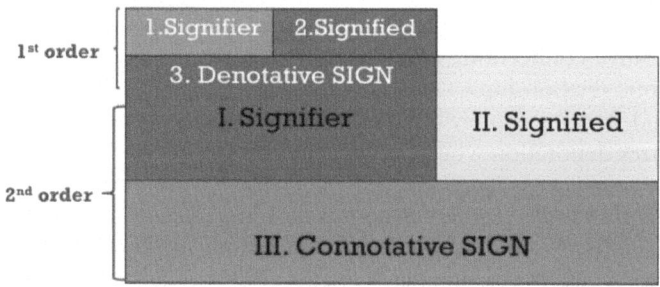

Fig. 3.4 Roland Barthes's first and second orders of significations

1972, p. 113). This formulation underlines the point that to determine the signifier and the signified, first, we need to know the level at which the analysis operates (see Fig. 3.4). This mechanism illustrates how signs can appear to signify one thing while carrying a multitude of meanings within their connotations.

For example, consider the name "Hollywood." It carries a multitude of connotations, invoking images of glitz, glamor, tinsel, celebrities, and the dreams of stardom. Simultaneously, "Hollywood" denotes a specific geographic area within Los Angeles, renowned as the epicenter of the American movie industry.

In the realm of semiotics, the alteration of a signifier while retaining the same signified can lead to diverse connotations. Changes in style or tone, such as employing distinct typefaces for identical text or shifting from sharp to soft focus in photography, can elicit varying connotations. This fluidity demonstrates how the manipulation of the signifier can alter the emotional and interpretational nuances of a message.

The selection of words also plays a pivotal role in invoking connotations. Consider the contrasting connotations in references to "strikes" versus "disputes," or "union demands" versus "management offers." These subtle shifts in terminology can frame a situation differently and influence how it is perceived.

Roland Barthes applied semiotic methods to unveil the myths that permeate various aspects of our lives, from media and fashion to art, photography, architecture, and literature. These myths aren't limited to classical fables of gods and heroes; they are pervasive narratives that shape our understanding of the world. Barthes' work sheds light on the power

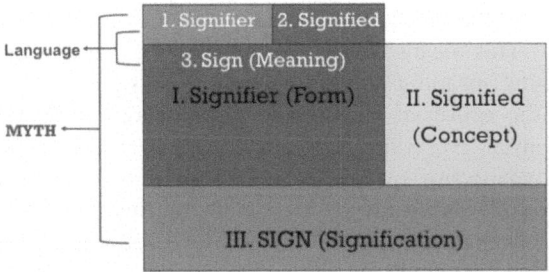

Fig. 3.5 Roland Barthes's orders of significations: language and myth

of signs and the intricate interplay between denotation and connotation in our everyday experiences (see Fig. 3.5).

Barthes's exploration of myths as the prevailing ideologies of our era sheds light on the intricate interplay of denotation and connotation that gives rise to these ideologies. In essence, these two orders of signification combine to create what Barthes labels as ideology. In the realm of myth, the signifier takes on the name "form," while the signified is referred to as a "concept." Notably, this "form" already encompasses a fully loaded sign, inherited from the cultural context, resulting in two levels of signification. Myth essentially operates as a "metalanguage," a language that conveys a message by utilizing pre-existing linguistic and cultural elements.

According to Barthes (1972), anything within a culture can function as a sign, conveying a specific message or concept. In his book, *Mythologies*, Barthes delineates various methods for "deciphering" these encoded messages within myths.

An example of a mythical discourse is found on the cover of "Paris-Match", where a black soldier is depicted giving the French salute. At the primary level (connotation viewpoint), the meaning is straightforward: "a black soldier performing the French salute." This meaning is conveyed through the visual representation of the soldier's specific gesture. However, it's at the secondary level (denotation point of view) that the myth unveils its ideological depth, which is "France is a great Empire, and all serve it without racial discrimination" ("French imperiality") (Barthes, 1972, p. 115).

This illustration showcases how myths operate within our culture, cloaking ideological messages within seemingly straightforward and innocuous signs.

Myth is a "system of communication" or a "message," a "mode of signification." This means that everything can be a myth, provided that it conveys some meaning or message (cultural signs and icons). Since language is the universal method of human communication, we can potentially convert everything into a language (Barthes, 1972).

Barthes's perspective on myth as a "system of communication" or a "message" underscores the broad scope of this concept. Essentially, anything possessing the capacity to convey meaning or a message, utilizing cultural signs and icons, can be viewed as a myth. In this context, myth transcends the conventional understanding of narratives and extends to the mundane elements of everyday life.

Roland Barthes's Theory of Semioclasm

Roland Barthes, in the preface to the 1970 edition of his book *Mythologies*, introduced a new term, *"semioclasm"* (Barthes, 1970).

Semioclasm refers to the practice of challenging and breaking down established social and cultural norms, conventions, and values. According to to Barthes, society is structured around a set of dominant ideologies, beliefs, and practices that are often taken for granted and accepted as natural. *Semioclasm* seeks to destabilize these dominant structures and expose the underlying power dynamics and social hierarchies (Barthes, 1970).

Building upon Roland Barthes's concept of *semioclasm*, the term *semioclast* refers to an individual or group who actively engages in the practice of breaking down established social and cultural norms. Semioclasts challenge dominant ideologies, beliefs, and practices, and seek to reveal how these structures serve to maintain social inequality and oppression (Barthes, 1970).

Semioclasts can take various forms, encompassing political activists, social justice advocates, artists, and writers who utilize their work to subvert dominant cultural codes and symbols. They may engage in direct action, protest, or civil disobedience to disrupt the status quo and challenge the prevailing power structures of society.

Semioclasm is not merely about rejecting or opposing established social norms but involves revealing their constructed nature and exposing how they serve to maintain social inequality and oppression. Semioclasm includes the deconstruction of cultural codes and symbols to unveil their hidden meanings and subtexts.

A semioclast is someone who directs their critical gaze toward the diverse sign systems that Barthes referred to as "collective representations" (Barthes, 1970), which had acquired the status of a myth. In other words, a *semioclast* is someone who attempts to dismantle the illusion created by our associations between signs and ideas.

For example, someone who points out that "security" often means being controlled, or that needing Nike swooshes to perform well at sports will always be for the biggest losers of all.

It's important to note that Barthes never presented mythology as the pure opposite of fact. To put it in the simplest terms, for Barthes, myth-making emerged from the desire for eternal principles or categories that somehow provided a form of psychological relief from divergent and contingent facts, experiences, and uncertainties of a single life.

We might think, for example, of a binary struggle between "Good and Evil," or forms of absolutist faith in institutions such as "the Church," "the Family," "the Party," "the Race," or "the Nation" (Biltoft, 2020).

Biltoft (2020) emphasizes that the issue doesn't lie in considering categories or institutions as fundamentally flawed. Instead, the key is to stay mindful and receptive to the potential of these categories to inadvertently foster rigid and inflexible modes of thinking, along with corresponding sets of behavioral norms.

For instance, one could reflect on how conventional notions of the family often rationalize particular gender roles, how racial ideologies legitimize discrimination, how strict religious doctrines establish an inflexible framework for evaluating conduct, or how political affiliations may require unwavering allegiance at the expense of individual discernment (Biltoft, 2020).

From this perspective, Roland Barthes (Barthes, 1970) turned the tools of semiology—the study of signs and their usage and interpretation—onto the human tendency to attach transcendental meaning to almost anything. Every fact could always be read as bound to and reflective of a web-like system of multi-sided meanings. Read carefully, Barthes's text is scattered with well-positioned lookouts, which offer different perspectives on current conflicts over how best to discover and then safeguard the truth.

In his book *Mythologies* (1972), Barthes speaks of wrestling ("le catch") in precisely these terms. Barthes claims that, in the United States, the formulaic violence of such spectacles offers audiences an Armageddon in miniature—the ultimate battle between good and evil neatly confined to a ring and fought by muscular, costumed proxies. As Barthes argues, "What is thus displayed for the public is the great spectacle of Suffering, Defeat, and Justice" (Barthes, 1972, p. 17). The dramaturgy of professional wrestling, by contrast, offers the catharsis-like effects that life lacks. Again and again, a caricatured combatant, after the much-choreographed struggle, eventually pins another to the ground.

The point for Barthes, however, is not only to understand the beating heart of wrestling. Rather, he sets out to decipher that spectacle as part of a broader effort to reveal the continued presence and power of myth in the modern world.

On this point, Barthes also provided more patently historical examples: "A French general pins a decoration on a one-armed Senegalese, a nun hands a cup of tea to a bed-ridden Arab, a white schoolmaster teaches attentive piccaninnies; the press undertakes every day to demonstrate that the store of mythical signifiers is inexhaustible" (Barthes, 1972, p. 123).

In each of these cases, the French Empire expresses itself in the symbolic garb of "Humanity" or "Civilization," and so reduces each subject to the symbolic dramaturgy of receiving the fruits of progress.

Barthes's concept of myth is particularly relevant for our era of misinformation, which tends to feed and foment conspiracy theories of all kinds. This is very close to Barthes' view that the power of myth rests in its ability to offer up eternal categories that help us feel confident, secure, and even in some way immortal. Thus, this craving for peace of mind can override any quest for "facts"—mentally destabilizing as they can be.

In other words, myth is a way of making facts correspond in some absolute way with a normative system of meaning. Let's look at the example from the study *"Social Media and Fake News in the 2016 Election"* by Hunt Allcott and Matthew Gentzkow to explain the above-mentioned specific of Barthes's myth: "The study has shown that a list of fake news websites, on which just over half of articles appear to be false, received 159 million visits during the month of the election, or 0.64 per US adult... Democrats and Republicans are both about 15 percent more likely to believe ideologically aligned headlines, and this ideologically aligned inference is substantially stronger for people with ideologically segregated social networks" (Allcott & Gentzkow, 2017, p. 113).

Application of Roland Barthes's Theory of Myth
Roland Barthes' theory of myth has been applied to a wide range of cultural phenomena, including advertising, media, and popular culture.

In recent years, his ideas have also been used to analyze the rise of fake news and misinformation in the digital age.

According to Barthes, myths are cultural narratives or symbols that have been transformed and naturalized to the point where they are taken for granted as truth (Barthes, 1972). In the context of fake news and misinformation, myths can be seen as false narratives or stories that have been deliberately spread to promote a particular agenda or belief.

One application of Barthes's theory of myth to fake news and misinformation analysis is the identification of the underlying ideology or worldview that a particular story or piece of information promotes. This involves analyzing the language, symbols, and narratives used in the story to uncover the hidden assumptions and values that it promotes (Barthes, 1972).

Another application of Barthes' theory of myth to fake news and misinformation analysis is the identification of ways in which these stories and pieces of information are spread and disseminated. This involves analyzing the channels and platforms through which they are distributed, as well as the social and cultural contexts in which they are shared and consumed.

By using Barthes's theory of myth to analyze fake news and misinformation, it is possible to expose the constructed nature of these narratives and reveal the hidden agendas and interests that they promote. This can help to promote critical thinking and media literacy and to counter the spread of false information and propaganda in the digital age.

An example of how Barthes' theory of myth can be applied to the analysis of fake news and misinformation is the spread of conspiracy theories related to the COVID-19 pandemic. One example of such a conspiracy theory is the claim that the virus was deliberately created and spread by the Chinese government as a form of biological warfare.

Using Barthes' theory of myth, we can analyze this conspiracy theory as a myth that has been constructed and naturalized to the point where it is taken for granted as truth by some people. The myth relies on many linguistic and symbolic codes, such as the use of military and scientific language to create a sense of urgency and credibility, and the framing of the Chinese government as a sinister and secretive force.

By analyzing how this myth is disseminated, we can also uncover the social and cultural contexts that allow it to spread. For example, social media platforms and online communities may provide echo chambers that reinforce and amplify the myth, while distrust of government and the media may make people more susceptible to believing in conspiracy theories.

By applying Barthes' theory of myth to the analysis of the above conspiracy theory, we can reveal the constructed nature of the myth and the hidden interests and agendas that it promotes. This can help to promote critical thinking and media literacy and counter the spread of false information and propaganda related to the COVID-19 pandemic.

The application of Barthes' theory of myth to fake news and misinformation analysis highlights the importance of understanding how cultural narratives and symbols shape our understanding of the world around us and the ways in which false information can be deliberately spread and manipulated for political or ideological purposes.

Algirdas Julien Greimas and Joseph Courtés Theory of Veridictory Square

The other important representatives of the dyadic theory of sign, whose concept of the *veridictory square* is widely used for analyses of fake news, are Algirdas Julien Greimas and Joseph Courtés. The theory of sign introduces the veridictory square as a valuable tool for analyzing the intricate relationships within a discourse. This conceptual framework delves into the dynamics of veridiction, exploring the interplay between truth and falseness in semiotic acts, such as textual communication (Greimas, 1987).

The veridictory square essentially represents the opposition of being/seeming projected onto the semiotic square, as described by Hébert and Tabler (2019, p. 10). This opposition provides a structured approach to dissecting the layers of meaning within a given text. By employing the veridictory square, analysts can unravel the complexities of signifying elements and discern the nuanced dynamics of truth and falsehood embedded in the semiotic fabric.

The factors (signifying elements) it takes into account are the following:

1. *The observing subject (S1, S2, etc.)*: The observing subject refers to the individual or group observing the object or discourse being analyzed (Hébert & Tabler, 2019, p. 10). Subjects bring their own perspectives, biases, and cultural contexts to the analysis, impacting the interpretation of signs and symbols.

2. The *object being observed* (*O1, O2, etc.*): This refers to the discourse or text being analyzed, including literary texts, political speeches, or visual art (Hébert & Tabler, 2019, p. 10). Identifying the object helps researchers analyze how signs and symbols are used within a specific context.

3. The *characteristic* of the *object Being Observed* (*C1, C2, etc.*): This factor is crucial in the veridictory square of Greimas and Courtés' concept. Characteristics may include verifiability, consistency with known facts, or conformity with social norms (Hébert & Tabler, 2019, p. 10).

4. Markers for *seeming* and *being* (*M1, M2*): M1 is the marker for seeming, suggesting that something is not what it appears to be. M2 is the marker for being, confirming that something is what it appears to be. Identifying these markers helps analyze language and discourse structure (Hébert & Tabler, 2019, p. 10).

5. The *four terms: being, seeming, not-being*, and *not-seeming*: These terms are arranged to create different relationships, enabling the analysis of statements in a text and identification of contradictions or inconsistencies (Hébert & Tabler, 2019, p. 10).

6. The *four metaterms* (or *compound terms*): These define the *veridictory* categories (Hébert & Tabler, 2019, p. 10):

   a. *True* or *truth* (*being + seeming*): Affirms existence and appearance.

   b. *Illusory* or *lie* (*not-being + seeming*): Denies existence, suggests an appearance/reality gap.

   c. *False* or *falsehood* (*not-being + not-seeming*): Denies existence and denies any suggestion of truth.

   d. *Secret* or *dissimulation* (*being + not-seeming*): Affirms existence but suggests it is not what it appears to be.

7. The *object's position* on the *square* (1, 2, 3, 4): Assigning a number based on its relationship to the four categories, helping to identify contradictions or inconsistencies (Hébert & Tabler, 2019, p. 10):

   Position 1—Truth (being + seeming): This position represents the assertion of truth or the genuine nature of an object. When an object occupies this position, it signifies a claim or representation that aligns with reality and factual accuracy. Analysts assign the number 1 to objects in this category, emphasizing the adherence to truth and the absence of distortion.

Position 2—Falsehood (not-being + not-seeming): Objects positioned here convey falsehood or an assertion that diverges from reality. When an object is placed in this category, it implies a departure from truth, introducing elements of fabrication, misinformation, or distortion. The number 2 is assigned to denote the deviation from truth and the presence of falseness.

Position 3—Secret (being + not-seeming): Objects in this position project an appearance of falseness, yet upon closer inspection, they align with reality. Assigned the number 3, this category indicates instances where the initial impression may be deceptive, but the object, upon thorough examination, proves to be truthful. It underscores the importance of scrutinizing apparent falsities for hidden truths.

Position 4—Lie (not-being + seeming): This position involves objects that present themselves as truthful but may carry elements of deception or misrepresentation. Assigned the number 4, this category suggests a semblance of truth, making it a critical area for analysis. It highlights instances where an object may appear genuine but requires scrutiny to uncover underlying inaccuracies.

8. *Time* (T): Represents the temporal aspect of the veridictory square. It includes time represented in the story, narrative time, and tactical time (Hébert & Tabler, 2019, p. 10).

These factors provide a comprehensive framework for analyzing language, discourse, and the construction of meaning within a given context.

Application of Greimas and Courtés Theory of Veridictory Square
The *veridictory square* can be a useful tool for analyzing fake news, as it provides a framework for understanding the different ways in which language can be used to shape reality.

For the purpose of fake news analysis using veridictory *square*, it's important to identify the markers for seeming and being (M1, M2) in the language being used. This can help to determine whether the language is presenting something as it appears to be (seeming) or as it actually is (being). In the case of fake news, the language may use markers for seeming in order to present false or misleading information as if it were true.

1. *Being* (*true* or *truth*): In the context of fake news, being can refer to statements or claims that are true. This could include accurate information that has been taken out of context or manipulated in some way to create a false impression. For example, a fake news story might include a fact (true) about a political figure's past but use it in a way that is misleading or deceptive.

2. *Seeming* (*illusory* or *lie seeming*) can refer to statements or claims that are presented as true but are actually false or misleading. This is the core of fake news, as it involves intentionally spreading false information to influence people's beliefs or actions. Seeming can also include the use of propaganda techniques to manipulate emotions and create a false sense of urgency or importance around a particular issue.

3. *Not-being* (*false* or *falsehood*) Not-being can refer to statements or claims that are untrue, with no basis in fact. This can include completely fabricated stories or events, as well as false statements about people, organizations, or events. Not-being can also include the use of misinformation or disinformation, which involves deliberately spreading false or misleading information in order to sow confusion or undermine trust in legitimate sources of information.

4. *Not-seeming* (*secret* or *dissimulation*): Not-seeming can refer to information that is deliberately kept hidden or obscured in order to create a false impression. This can include the use of selective or biased reporting to shape public perception of events, as well as the deliberate suppression of information that would contradict a particular narrative. Not-seeming can also include the use of dog-whistle language or coded messaging to appeal to certain groups without overtly stating a particular position or belief.

Using the veridictory square, researchers can also examine the relationship between language and reality and identify where fake news falls within the framework.

The four terms and metaterms of the veridictory square can be applied to the language being analyzed. Fake news may fall into the category of illusion or falsehood, which is characterized by not-being and/or not-seeming. This means that the information being presented is not true and maybe intentionally misleading or deceptive.

Tactical time can also be analyzed in the context of fake news. For instance, some fake news stories may use misleading headlines or misleading images to grab attention and generate clicks, even if the content of the story itself is not accurate. These tactics can be used to manipulate the reader's perception of reality and create a false sense of urgency or importance around a particular topic.

For example, let's say there is a fake news story claiming that a famous politician has been involved in a major scandal. We can use the veridictory square to analyze the story as follows:

1. Markers for *seeming* and *being* (*M1, M2*): The story is presented in a way that seems to be true, with details and quotes from supposed sources. However, the sources are anonymous and unverified, and there is no concrete evidence presented to support the claims. Therefore, the story only seems to be true, but not necessarily true.

2. Four terms: The story can be analyzed in terms of its veridictory status, as follows:

   • *Being*: The story is being presented as true and accurate.
   • *Seeming*: The story only seems to be true, as there is no concrete evidence to support the claims.
   • *Not-being*: The story is *not-being* true, as there is no concrete evidence to support the claims.
   • *Not-seeming*: The story is *not-seeming* false, as it is presented in a way that seems to be true but is not necessarily so.

3. *Four metaterms*: The story can also be analyzed in terms of the four veridictory categories, as follows:

   • *True* or *truth* (*being* + *seeming*): In the realm of fake news, this metaterm might be applicable when a story is presented as true, yet it only seems to be so. The intention here could be to mislead the audience into believing misinformation.
   • *Illusory* or *lie* (*not-being* + *seeming*): Fake news often falls into this category, as it involves intentional deception. The story is presented in a way that seems true, but it is intentionally fabricated or misleading.
   • *False* or *falsehood* (*not-being* + *not-seeming*): When a story lacks concrete evidence to support its claims, it can be categorized as false. This aligns with the skepticism inherent in evaluating fake news, as it often lacks verifiable evidence.

- *Secret* or *dissimulation* (*being* + *not-seeming*): In the context of fake news, this metaterm might describe a situation where the falsehood is not overtly apparent. The story is being presented in a way that may not necessarily seem false at first glance, but closer scrutiny reveals the deception.

4. *Object's position on the square*: Based on the above analysis, the story's position on the veridictory square would be in the category of not-being + seeming (lie, position 4), as there is no concrete evidence to support the claims made in the story.

5. *Time* (*T*): The use of time in analyzing the veridictory status of the story would depend on the specific details of the story. For example, if the story claims that the scandal occurred in the past, then the representation of time in the story would be important to consider. Additionally, the use of narrative time and tactical time in the story could also have an impact on how the story is perceived by readers or listeners.

It is important to note that a veridictory evaluation using the veridictory square is always subject to relativization. This means that the veridictory status of a story may vary depending on different perspectives, contexts, and criteria.

For example, a story that is deemed false based on concrete evidence may be considered true by someone who has a strong bias or agenda. Similarly, a story that is presented in a way that seems to be true may be seen as not seeming true by someone who is skeptical or critical of the sources.

Furthermore, the veridictory square is not a fixed or objective measure of truth or falsehood, but rather a tool for analyzing the veridictory status of a story based on specific criteria and assumptions. Different criteria or assumptions may lead to different evaluations of the same story.

Therefore, it is important to approach veridictory evaluations with a critical and open-minded perspective and to consider the limitations and potential biases of the analysis. It is also important to gather information and evidence from multiple sources and perspectives and to be aware of the potential impact of media and online platforms on the veridictory status of information.

Triadic Model of the Sign

Charles Saunders Peirce's Semiotic Theory

Charles Saunders Peirce's Model of the Sign

At around the same time as Saussure was formulating his model of the sign, across the Atlantic independent work was also in progress as the pragmatist philosopher and logician Charles Sanders Peirce formulated his own model of the sign. In contrast to Saussure's model of the sign in the form of a "self-contained dyad," Peirce offered a triadic model (Chandler, 1994).

In Peirce's framework, a sign, also known as a *representamen*, is not a standalone entity but rather a component of a process involving three subjects: the sign itself, its object, and its interpretant. The term "semiosis" is central to Peirce's concept, defining it as the process of language signification. Please note that the interpretant is not an interpreter but rather the sense made of the sign (Chandler, 1994).

According to Charles Peirce (1958), a sign, in the form of a repre-sentamen, serves as a means of conveying meaning. It is something that stands for something else in a particular context or capacity. The *representamen* is the actual form in which the sign manifests, such as spoken or written words. It is directed toward someone and has the power to generate an equivalent or even a more elaborate sign within the mind of another individual. This subsequent sign, created as a result of the original one, is referred to as the *interpretant* by Peirce. In essence, this concept highlights the intricate nature of communication and the role of signs in conveying meaning to others (Peirce, 1958).

To break it down further, let's consider the example of a traffic light sign that signals "stop." Within Peirce's model, this sign can be analyzed as follows:

1. The *representamen*: This is the form in which the sign appears like the red light facing the traffic at an intersection. It's the visual or symbolic aspect of the sign.
2. The *object*: This refers to what the sign is pointing to or repre-senting. In this case, it's the action of vehicles halting when they encounter the red light. The object is the real-world reference that the sign relates to.

3. The *interpretant*: This is where the meaning and sense of the sign comes into play. When individuals see the red light, they interpret it as an indication that vehicles must stop. In other words, the interpretant is the mental or cognitive response to the sign.

Peirce's triadic model underscores the dynamic nature of signs, existing in a continuous process of interpretation and meaning-making. It recognizes that signs are not static but evolve as they are understood and applied by individuals.

This model's emphasis on the interpretant as the sense made of the sign highlights the importance of the receiver's role in shaping the meaning of signs. It offers a valuable perspective on how communication and language function in a complex and interconnected way.

Peirce (1958), clearly fascinated by tripartite structures, made a phenomenological distinction between the sign itself (or the representamen) as an instance of firstness, its object as an instance of secondness, and the interpretant as an instance of thirdness.

Firstness in Peirce's framework is a realm of pure potential and emotion. It's a space of indescribable feelings that exist independently of concrete objects. Imagine the feeling of "yellow-ness" or any other emotion that arises without a direct reference to something in the external world. Firstness is like a canvas of raw, unstructured emotions, somewhat akin to the unspoken sensations one might experience during meditation when contemplating a simple, flickering candle flame.

Secondness represents the object in the semiotic process. It's the moment when the sign interacts with a concrete entity or event in the external world. Simply put, it is the juncture at which an abstract sign, such as the notion of "yellow-ness," intersects with a real, yellow object like a sunflower. This encounter establishes a connection between the abstract and the tangible.

Thirdness takes this a step further by introducing the concept of interpretation. It's the realm where a sign, its object, and the mental associations and meanings associated with it are brought together. Thirdness is where the concept of "yellow-ness" becomes linked with the emotional response, knowledge, and shared understanding of what yellow represents.

In the context of fake news and misinformation, firstness can be seen as the initial creation or fabrication of false narratives or misleading information. This may involve intentionally distorting or exaggerating the truth or creating entirely fictitious stories to promote a particular agenda or viewpoint.

Secondness is the mode of being that is in relation to something else. Secondness is the level of consciousness where the idea of "reality" comes into play. While firstness is about being, secondness is about the existence of some experiential universe. Secondness manifests itself when firstness relates to another object through relation, compulsion, effect, dependence, independence, negation, occurrence, result, or reality. For instance, the firstness of the quality of "redness," when attributed to a red rose, becomes secondness. For example, one can perceive or imagine the rose's specific odor.

In the context of fake news and misinformation, secondness can be seen as the dissemination and reception of false information by individuals or groups. This may involve individuals sharing false stories on social media or consuming and believing false information without verifying its accuracy.

Thirdness is the mediator through which a first and a second are brought into relation. "Thirdness" of the intellectual mood is a result of cultural socialization, social conventions, and rules. Here, the interpretant becomes a third element between the sign and the object. Third is a bridge between the First and the Second. According to Peirce (1958), thirdness is a synthetic consciousness driven by the sense of learning, thought, memory, and habit.

In the context of fake news and misinformation, thirdness can be seen as the broader impact and consequences of false information on society. This may include the perpetuation of harmful stereotypes, the erosion of trust in media and democratic institutions, or even the incitement of violence or social unrest.

Charles Sanders Peirce's semiotic theory encompasses a vast array of sign typologies and offers over 76 distinct definitions of what constitutes a sign. While this multiplicity of definitions can seem daunting, some canonical typologies serve as fundamental cornerstones in understanding the concept of signs. One crucial distinction in Peirce's framework is the categorization into *indexes*, *icons*, and *symbols* (Chandler, 1994).

Indexes, often referred to as indexicals, establish a direct and tangible connection between the representamen, and the object. This connection can be physical or causal and is either observable or inferable. Consider "natural signs," which are prime examples of indexes: phenomena like smoke, thunder, footprints, echoes, and even non-synthetic odors and flavors. These signs provide immediate, concrete evidence of the objects they represent, making them compelling examples of indexicality.

"Signals" such as knocking on a door, a ringing phone, or personal "trademarks" like handwriting or a distinctive catchphrase also fall under the indexical category. In each case, there's a clear and direct connection between the sign and its referent, be it through physical causation or direct inference.

In the domain of fake news, indexical signs often involve deceptive elements like misleading statistics, quotes taken out of context, or doctored images and videos. Consider a scenario where a politician selectively cites a statistic out of context to reinforce a false narrative, creating a persuasive yet inaccurate impression. This approach can be especially convincing for those who neglect to verify the original source, emphasizing the crucial role of fact-checking and critical evaluation in navigating today's complex information landscape.

The concept of *icon* within Peirce's theory of semiotics denotes a mode wherein the representamen is perceived as resembling or imitating the object. This resemblance is evident through recognizable visual, auditory, tactile, gustatory, or olfactory qualities, creating a semblance that mirrors the essence of the original. Examples of this mode abound, including portraits, cartoons, scale models, the sound of a launching application, auditory effects in radio dramas, dubbed film soundtracks, and imitative gestures (Chandler, 1994). Through these instances, the *icon* serves as a vivid representation that captures and echoes the inherent characteristics of the object it signifies.

In the sphere of fake news and misinformation, iconic signs often encompass manipulated visuals, such as edited images or videos, designed to create a false impression or support a misleading narrative. For instance, an image of a crowded protest might be altered to exaggerate or diminish the crowd size, catering to a specific agenda. In the digital age, these *iconic signs* wield significant influence, highlighting the imperative of media literacy and critical discernment for an informed public.

The concept of *symbol* in the context of Peirce's semiotics delineates a mode where the representamen lacks resemblance to the object and is inherently arbitrary or convention-based, necessitating a learned relationship. Examples encompass various forms of language (alphabetical letters, punctuation marks, words, phrases, and sentences), numbers, Morse code, traffic lights, and national flags (Chandler, 1994). This mode underscores the significance of cultural and societal agreements, emphasizing the need for education in deciphering these symbolic systems.

In the context of fake news, symbolic signs often involve language or narratives strategically leveraging cultural or political biases and prejudices. Consider a false narrative targeting a specific ethnic or religious group, relying on symbolic language and imagery to perpetuate stereotypes, even if the narrative is entirely false. This manipulation highlights the potency of symbolic signs in shaping public opinion, urging a critical examination of the narratives presented and reinforcing the importance of media literacy.

The three forms are listed here in increasing order of conventionality. Symbolic signs, exemplified by language, are highly conventional; iconic signs inherently involve some degree of conventionality; and indexical signs "direct attention to their objects by blind compulsion" (Peirce, 1931, p. 306). This progression underscores that symbolic signs rely extensively on established conventions, while iconic signs exhibit varying degrees of conventionality, and indexical signs compel attention directly, emphasizing the nuanced spectrum of semiotic expression and its role in communication.

Charles Saunders Peirce's Belief Fixation Methods

In exploring fake news through Peirce's semiotic lens, we examine the intricate influence that beliefs exert and scrutinize the notion of an external reality accurately mirrored in news narratives.

As previously discussed, according to Peirce, reality stands independently of individual perceptions, acting upon our thoughts and generating ideas in harmony with them. However, reality itself remains an external, dynamic entity rather than an immediate object of thought. The potential connection between thought and reality instills hope for reaching truth through a reasoned process.

Understanding this, we confront the challenge posed by fake news, where narratives may diverge from this ideal connection. Fake news often manipulates the semiotic relationship between signs and their referents, distorting the alignment between thought and external reality. This deviation underscores the importance of critical analysis and media literacy to navigate the complex interplay of semiotics in the dissemination of information.

Peirce's exploration of belief fixation in *The Fixation of Belief* (1877) introduces four methods: the *method of tenacity, authority, a priori reasoning*, and the *scientific method*.

The *method of tenacity* is depicted as an unwavering adherence to personal beliefs, akin to an ostrich burying its head in the sand to avoid confronting contradictory evidence. This resonates with modern online discourse, particularly on platforms like Facebook, where polarized discussions thrive. In these virtual arenas, individuals tenaciously cling to their beliefs despite the complexity of the issues (Franco, 2017).

Franco (2017) notes the prevalence of this tenacity, especially in politically charged contexts, where individuals find psychological comfort in unwavering commitment to their ideas. The method efficiently prompts immediate and decisive actions while shielding individuals from the discomfort of uncertainty.

Understanding the belief fixation method is crucial for dissecting real-world discourse dynamics. Peirce's insights illuminate how conviction, resistance to contradiction, and the pursuit of psychological comfort manifest in contemporary discussions.

The *method of authority*, in Peirce's examination, plays a significant role, influencing beliefs within communities through institutions that uphold specific dogmas and suppress the establishment of new ones (Franco, 2017). This approach involves individuals adopting beliefs dictated by those in power, restricting freedom as institutions seek to shape minds according to their interpretations of reality.

On platforms like Facebook, manifestations of this belief system are evident, particularly in discussions revolving around religious debates and political viewpoints (Franco, 2017). The influence of authoritative figures or institutions is apparent, contributing to the collective beliefs within these online communities.

An illuminating case is President Trump's dismissal of "CNN as 'fake' and Fox News as 'real'" (Schwartz, 2018), highlighting the intersection of political interests with the interpretation of facts presented by media outlets. This example underscores the pervasive influence of authoritative figures, emphasizing the importance of comprehending how beliefs are structured and disseminated within societal frameworks.

The *a priori method* solidifies beliefs deemed agreeable to reason. In practical terms, individuals tend to gravitate toward ideas that resonate with their existing convictions. Narratives aligning with preconceived beliefs are often embraced as true, irrespective of their correspondence with lived experiences. This psychological tendency is commonly acknowledged as confirmation bias (Gorman & Gorman, 2016; Kolbert, 2017), although Mercier and Sperber (2017) prefer the term myside bias.

These scholars underscore a noteworthy phenomenon where individuals derive genuine pleasure from encountering information that supports their pre-existing beliefs, even when these beliefs are objectively incorrect. This inclination illuminates the dynamics observed in filter bubbles and echo chambers on social media platforms, a prominent example being Facebook.

Facebook utilizes algorithms to filter and organize information, prioritizing content that aligns with an individual's preferences. Employing the *a priori method* in information selection, Facebook, a major global news source (Reuters Institute, 2017), tends to shield users from conflicting viewpoints, fostering a false sense of overall agreement with their beliefs. This curated information contributes to users' peace of mind and satisfaction, reinforcing their reluctance to entertain conflicting opinions and potentially challenge their established beliefs.

This desire for cognitive consonance often prevails, leading individuals to seek information that reaffirms their existing worldview. The comfort derived from confirmation, even if it means being insulated from diverse perspectives, exemplifies the profound impact of the a priori method on shaping belief systems. This dynamic interaction between information curation and individual beliefs underscores the complex interplay influencing how people perceive and engage with the world around them.

The last method presented by Peirce is the *scientific method*. Contrary to the tenacity method, in the scientific method, an individual opinion cannot be considered the truth, for truth is a shared opinion. The essence of this method is that it is repeatable by other inquirers, and if the method is properly followed, they should arrive at the same conclusion and hence the same belief. A common belief is based only on external events and shared by everyone.

The scientific method unfolds in a dual process. Initially, there's reasoning, where a belief begets other beliefs within the mind, devoid of external elements independent of thought. The subsequent step is observation, introducing external elements as a new belief emerges through scrutiny. Observations, unique in their essence, don't directly correspond to the event; instead, they are mental representations of the event. This duality encapsulates the dynamic interplay between internal reasoning and external observation, highlighting the intricate process by which beliefs evolve and align with empirical reality.

In this context, every news report (regardless of whether it is fake or not) involves the process of representation and, consequently, interpretation of reality. Journalistic reports, in the best-case scenario, bring us facts, the result of the reporter's observation of an event. Every news report is a particular observation of an event. The problem with the accuracy of news reports is that published reports are not necessarily the result of an investigative process based on reasoning and observation. A news media company may report what is a reiteration of what journalists at other media companies have written, without any effort to observe the original event or to gain collateral experience of it. This is one of the reasons for certain fake news reports being spread so quickly.

Charles Saunders Peirce's Principles of Association
Peirce's semiotics, with its profound emphasis on the connection between thought and reality, stands as a potent framework for dissecting the menace of fake news and devising strategies to combat it. In Peirce's (1932) view, a sign triggers a sequence of thoughts in the mind, governed by three fundamental principles—or habits of thought—that link one idea to another within this cognitive chain.

1. The *principle of resemblance* is the feeling or the sense of similar qualities in which similar ideas come one after the other without any consideration or consciousness of the process. This automatic succession underscores the subtle yet potent influence of associations on thought processes.
2. The *principle of contiguity* is based on proximity in time or space. It involves the recognition of something that calls attention, connecting stimuli that captivate our attention to a quality through a proposition. This principle highlights the pivotal role of attention and conscious engagement in shaping our cognitive understanding.
3. The *principle of causality* refers to the association of ideas based on their cause-and-effect relationship. It manifests as an association of ideas imbued with a sense of learning, operating as an inference that provides a comprehensive description. It goes beyond mere representation; it asserts that through contemplation of its premises, additional insights about the subject can be gleaned.

The third principle is the association of ideas that brings with it the sense of learning, working like an inference that contains a general description and purports to represent the fact (Peirce, 1932). It does even more; it professes to give in its premises such a representation of the fact that by contemplation of them, something else may be learned about the thing.

As the third principle intricately involves the other two, successful representation can only evoke an idea in the mind when the two preceding conditions are satisfied. Moreover, it becomes imperative to associate the inherent qualities of the sign itself, which might not necessarily relate to its meaning, with the external objects that cause the sign. This association is crucial to attain an inference that serves as the synthesis of the entire cognitive process, bridging the gap between the sign and its meaningful interpretation in the external world.

In such a process, we pass from a particular to a general assertion. The apprehension of general laws suggests a future tendency, which is based on experience and feelings caused by events. If a general law is a law of mind, we may understand it as a habit of mind that will be created at the end of the inquiry process.

For instance, following an investigation, one reader of a particular newspaper article might perceive a given news report as a reliable representation of an event, while another might entirely discredit it. Such belief or disbelief holds the potential to significantly impact the reader's future actions. These actions may range from deciding whether to share the information or not, saving the link for further investigation, or even committing it to memory as a reference point to avoid future readings from that particular news source. The dynamic interplay between belief, skepticism, and subsequent actions underscores the profound influence of information processing on individual decision-making.

The complexity of fake news is closely tied to the algorithms underpinning social networks like Facebook. Personalization and tailored content mechanisms play a significant role, potentially giving rise to filter bubbles—digital algorithms selectively predict the information users want to see, causing intellectual isolation. Similarly, echo chambers can form, where closed media systems reinforce existing beliefs. This interaction between algorithmic logic and user experience highlights technology's substantial impact on information consumption, influencing perspectives and potentially contributing to polarization.

Everything counts not just social networks' agenda, which informed, for instance, the 2018 decision to prioritize family's and friends' news feed content over that from brands and media organizations (Chaykowski, 2018), but also whatever a user likes, loves, shares; whatever groups a user belongs to; who a user follows or unfollows; how often a user accesses a social network; from which device it is accessed; with which friends a user interacts most; and so forth. The logic of algorithms to personalize the content on search engines, news aggregators, and social networks such as Facebook therefore potentially creates filter bubbles and echo chambers that can lead to ideological segregation, the perpetuation of misinformation, and confirmation biases.

Echo chambers are formed when information, ideas, and/or beliefs are reinforced by repetition within a closed system. As "false information is fed into self-reinforcing algorithmic and cognitive systems, or digital 'echo chambers'" (Bakir & McStay, 2018, p. 161), it creates a fertile terrain for fake news to grow on social networks.

Peirce's three principles of association—*resemblance, contiguity*, and *causality*—provide a nuanced lens through which we can understand the intricate dynamics of information processing and belief formation. Examining the complexities of fake news within this framework reveals how our minds navigate through a network of ideas. The algorithmic landscape of social networks, with its personalized content and filter mechanisms, often intersects with these principles, contributing to the formation of filter bubbles and echo chambers. Recognizing and navigating these associations is crucial for fostering a more balanced and informed digital discourse, one that transcends the challenges posed by fake news and algorithmic influence.

Application of Charles Saunders Peirce's Semiotic Theory
In the context of fake news and misinformation, as mentioned above, Charles Saunders Peirce's principles of association (Peirce, 1932) provide a valuable framework for understanding and addressing the complexities inherent in the acceptance and dissemination of false narratives. These principles—*resemblance, contiguity*, and *causality*—offer a comprehensive perspective on the cognitive processes that contribute to the effectiveness of misleading information. Each principle provides a unique perspective that, when integrated, contributes to a more robust strategy for fostering critical thinking and resilience against the impact of false narratives:

1. *The principle of resemblance (sense of similar qualities)*:
   In the realm of fake news, misinformation often bears resemblance to factual information. This triggers a chain of thoughts that might lead individuals to accept the false narrative. For instance, misleading information about COVID might resemble accurate data, leading to automatic associations. An example of this resemblance could be the dissemination of inaccurate statistics or manipulated graphs that superficially mimic legitimate health data. In such cases, individuals might unknowingly accept the misleading information, assuming it aligns with the familiar patterns of authentic data.

2. *The principle of contiguity (proximity in time or space)*:
   Misinformation spreads swiftly due to its immediate relevance or proximity in time and space. Misleading information tends to spread rapidly on social media platforms due to the immediacy of the content. The proximity in time to significant events or news announcements amplifies the impact of false narratives, creating a sense of urgency or connection that captures the attention of a wide audience. For instance, during political events or public health emergencies, false information can quickly gain traction by piggybacking on the heightened awareness and emotions surrounding these occurrences.

3. *The principle of causality (cause-and-effect relationship)*:
   Misleading narratives often create a cause-and-effect relationship, constructing a persuasive yet inaccurate interpretation. For instance, contemporary misinformation about vaccines frequently fabricates a cause-and-effect perception, linking immunizations to unrelated health issues. Instances of false information incorrectly associating vaccines with severe side effects or enduring health risks, such as the claim that vaccination may cause autism, can instill doubts in individuals regarding the safety and effectiveness of vaccination initiatives. This misleading attribution has the potential to erode public confidence in vaccines, fostering vaccine hesitancy and potentially compromising the overall immunity of communities.

Charles William Morris's Semiotic Theory

Charles William Morris's Four Elements of Semiosis

Charles William Morris, an American philosopher and semiotician, made significant contributions to pragmatism and semiotics, building upon ideas initially formulated by Charles Sanders Peirce and other pragmatists. In his work *Signs, Language, and Behavior* (1946/1955), Morris aimed to synthesize and expand upon the diverse contributions of various pragmatist philosophers within the framework of semiotics, a field that focuses on the study of signs and symbols and their interpretation. Morris sought to provide a systematic approach to understanding the relationship between signs, language, and human behavior.

According to Morris (1946/1955), semiosis, the process of signification, involves four key components:

1. *Sign vehicle*: This refers to the physical form of the sign, such as an object or an event. The sign vehicle is the tangible element that carries the potential to convey meaning. For example, a written word, a gesture, or a sound could serve as a sign vehicle.
2. *Designatum*: The designatum is the kind of object or the class of objects that the sign is intended to designate or represent. It represents the conceptual category or meaning associated with the sign. For instance, if the sign vehicle is a red traffic light, the designatum could be the instruction to stop.
3. *Interpretant*: The interpretant is a crucial aspect of Morris's theory and involves the disposition of an interpreter to initiate a response sequence upon perceiving the sign. It's not just about recognizing the sign but also about the mental and behavioral response triggered by the sign. The interpretant is, in a way, the effect the sign has on the interpreter.
4. *Interpreter*: This component involves the person for whom the sign vehicle functions as a sign. The interpreter is the one who perceives the sign and processes its meaning. The interpretation of the sign is influenced by the individual's experiences, cultural background, and context.

According to Morris (1946/1955), every sign must have a designatum, or as he later referred to it, a significatum. The designatum is the conceptual category or class of objects that the sign is intended to represent, providing the sign with meaning and purpose.

However, Morris introduces an interesting nuance by pointing out that not every sign necessarily must have a denotatum. The denotatum, in semiotic terms, is the actual existing object or event in the external world that the sign points to or denotes. In simpler terms, a sign must designate something, indicating a conceptual category or meaning (designatum), but it doesn't always have to directly point to or denote a tangible, real-world object or event (Morris, 1971).

For instance, in the realm of mythology, if the sign "unicorn" is used to refer to its object as existent in the world of mythology, where unicorns are fantastical creatures, the sign indeed has a *denotatum*. In this context, the *denotatum* is the mythical existence of unicorns within the narrative of myths and legends. The sign successfully points to the conceptual category of mythical creatures, and thus, it has both a *designatum* (the category of mythical creatures) and a *denotatum* (the existence of unicorns within mythology) (Chandler, 1994).

Conversely, if the sign "*unicorn*" is used to refer to its object considering it as existent in the world of zoology, where zoology deals with the study of real, existing animals, then the sign does not have a *denotatum*. Unicorns, as creatures with a single horn on their heads, do not exist in the zoological world. However, the sign still retains a *designatum*, representing the conceptual category of mythical creatures, but without a corresponding *denotatum* in the realm of zoology (Chandler, 1994).

Charles William Morris's Syntax, Semantic, and Pragmatic Dimensions

Morris (1938) extends his semiotic framework to the study of language, emphasizing that language operates as a complex system of signs with distinct rules. He identifies three key dimensions that govern language: *syntactic*, *semantic*, and *pragmatic* rules.

1. *Syntactic rules*: Morris highlights the syntactic dimension of language, which concerns the formal structure and arrangement of signs within a linguistic system (Morris, 1938). Syntactic rules govern how signs, such as words and symbols, are combined to create meaningful expressions and sentences. This aspect is crucial for understanding the grammatical structure and syntax of a language.

2. *Semantic rules*: The semantic dimension of language, according to Morris (1938), focuses on the meaning of signs. Semantic rules govern how signs relate to the objects or concepts they represent. This dimension explores the connection between linguistic expressions and their intended or interpreted meanings, providing insight into the semantic richness of language.
3. *Pragmatic rules*: Morris (1938) introduces the pragmatic dimension, which deals with the practical use of signs in social contexts. Pragmatic rules govern how signs function in communication, taking into account the context, the intentions of speakers, and the responses of interpreters. This dimension delves into the dynamic nature of language use, emphasizing the role of communication in social interaction.

In other words, semiotics may be divided into three branches: *syntactics* or *syntax*, *semantics*, and *pragmatics*.

In other words, semiotics may be divided into three branches: *syntactics* or *syntax*, *semantics*, and *pragmatics*.

1. *Syntactics (Syntax)*: Syntactics is dedicated to describing the formal or structural relationships between signs, particularly focusing on sentence structure and the rules of grammar. It helps elucidate how words are organized to convey meaning. For instance, consider the stark contrast between the sentences "I robbed a bank" and "A bank robbed me." The difference in word order changes the entire meaning: the first implies the speaker took money from a bank, while the second suggests that the bank took money from the speaker. Understanding syntax is crucial for effective communication, as it ensures clarity and precision in conveying intended meanings (Brewer, 2020).
2. *Semantics*: Semantics explores the relationship of signs to what they stand for, studying the meanings of sentences. It's concerned with the understanding of words and their meanings within a linguistic context. An example provided illustrates this point: the sentence "A rabbit chased the dog through the pasture" might be syntactically correct but seems odd from a semantic perspective because, in reality, rabbits typically don't chase dogs. Semantics is essential for

grasping the nuances and subtleties of language, helping to convey accurate and meaningful messages (Brewer, 2020).

3. *Pragmatics*: Pragmatics explores the relationship of signs to inter-preters and studies the meanings of sentences within specific contexts. It goes beyond formal language structure and meaning, considering how language is used in real-life situations. An example like "Break it down" illustrates the importance of pragmatics, as the meaning of this declarative sentence depends on the context in which it is used. The meaning of this sentence changes dramat-ically with context. If you're at the end of a large gathering and someone tells you to "break it down," they may mean for you to help put away folding chairs and folding tables. On a dance floor, a person would logically hear "break it down" as a call to show off some super sweet dance moves. In a business presentation, "break it down" may be a call for you to share your great business-related concept (Brewer, 2020).

Concluding the above-mentioned points, syntax serves as the foun-dation for constructing language, semantics adds layers of meaning to our expressions, and pragmatics guides us in applying the appropriate meaning in diverse situations. Together, these elements create a compre-hensive framework for effective communication, allowing us to convey and interpret thoughts with nuance and precision.

Application of Charles William Morris's Semiotic Theory
In the context of fake news and misinformation, Morris's theory can help us understand how different social and cultural factors shape the creation and reception of false information.

The components of semiosis, including the sign vehicle, the desig-natum the interpretant, and the interpreter, can be applied to the analysis of media discourse to better understand how such content is created and interpreted:

1. *The sign vehicles* employed in fake news are diverse, encompassing various formats such as text, images, videos, and social media posts. Crafted with meticulous precision, these sign vehicles aim to resonate with the emotions and biases of their targeted audience, leveraging techniques that range from sensationalist headlines to

provocative images and intentionally misleading information. This strategic composition is designed to captivate attention, manipulating perceptions and fostering a response aligned with the creator's objectives. By scrutinizing these sign vehicles, one can unravel the intricate web of tactics used to deceive and influence the audience. A typical instance might involve a fake news story featuring a sensationalist headline like "Politician X Caught Red-Handed in Illegal Activity!" complemented by a doctored photo portraying the politician engaging in purportedly suspicious behavior. This multifaceted approach underscores the importance of dissecting the components of sign vehicles to discern the methods employed in the dissemination of deceptive narratives.

2. *The designatum* in the realm of fake news serves as the focal point, representing the type of object or class of objects that the sign aims to designate. Within the context of fake news, this designatum frequently manifests as a warped or magnified interpretation of reality, strategically crafted to evoke intense emotional responses such as fear, outrage, or indignation from the audience. A critical analysis of the designatum in fake news stories unveils the intricate layers of manipulation and sheds light on the often concealed ideological or political motives that underlie the content.

   A typical designatum in a fake news narrative involves the distortion or exaggeration of reality, strategically deployed to elicit strong emotional reactions. For instance, a fake news story might falsely assert that a politician was caught accepting bribes or engaging in corrupt activities, despite a lack of substantiating evidence. This deliberate distortion not only exemplifies the deceptive nature of fake news but also emphasizes the importance of scrutinizing the designatum to unveil the broader agenda that may be concealed behind the sensationalized content.

3. *The interpretant* in the context of fake news encapsulates the predisposition of an interpreter to initiate a response sequence upon perceiving the sign. In the deceptive realm of fake news, this *interpretant* often takes the form of potent emotional reactions, ranging from anger and fear to disgust. These deliberately evoked emotional responses play a pivotal role in the manipulation and deception orchestrated by the creators of fake news. Analyzing the interpretant of fake news stories unveils the intricate mechanisms employed to exploit the audience's emotional vulnerabilities.

For instance, in the mentioned fake news story, the interpretant could manifest as a powerful emotional response—be it anger, fear, or disgust—elicited by the fabricated allegations against the politician. The intentional cultivation of such emotional reactions serves as a tool for the creators of the fake news story to manipulate and deceive the audience effectively. Understanding the nuances of the interpretant in fake news allows for a deeper comprehension of how emotional triggers are strategically harnessed to shape perceptions and influence the audience's response to the misinformation presented.

4. *The interpreter* in the context of a fake news story often represents a member of a specific political or ideological group, whose existing beliefs and values are strategically reinforced by the content. In this intricate dynamic, the fake news narrative is crafted not only to deceive but also to resonate with the perspectives of the targeted audience. For instance, the story may be meticulously designed to appeal to individuals who already harbor a deep distrust for the implicated politician or who hold negative views about the political party the politician represents.

In the given example, the interpreter could be someone with pre-existing doubts or negative sentiments towards the politician, and the fake news story becomes a potent tool to validate and intensify those sentiments. By aligning the content with the interpreter's preconceived beliefs, fake news creators exploit the interpreter's cognitive biases, fostering a sense of affirmation and reinforcing existing opinions. Analyzing the *interpreter* of fake news thus provides insight into the strategic use of content to bolster and amplify pre-existing beliefs and biases within specific political or ideological factions. This manipulation of interpretation underscores the broader impact of fake news on shaping individual perspectives and influencing group dynamics.

In the realm of fake news and misinformation, the application of semiotics, comprising syntactics, semantics, and pragmatics, offers a nuanced understanding of how signs are structured, convey meaning, and interact within specific contexts.

1. *Syntactics (Syntax)*: In the syntactical dimension, the focus lies on the formal and structural relationships between signs, emphasizing sentence structure and grammatical rules. This is pivotal in the analysis of fake news, where the manipulation of syntax can drastically alter the perceived meaning of a statement. Consider the sentences "The politician exposed corruption" and "Exposed, the politician's corruption." The manipulation of word order in these syntactically valid sentences can influence how readers interpret the information, showcasing the importance of syntactics in crafting persuasive narratives.

2. *Semantics*: The exploration of semantics is crucial in deciphering the meanings of signs and their representations. In the context of fake news, the careful selection and interpretation of words play a central role in misleading or influencing the audience. For instance, a headline stating "Scientific Breakthrough Cures Disease" may, in reality, be a semantic manipulation, leading readers to believe in a groundbreaking discovery that may not align with the scientific consensus. Semantics, therefore, aids in unraveling the subtleties of language used to convey inaccurate or deceptive messages.

3. *Pragmatics*: Pragmatics explores the relationship between signs and interpreters within specific contexts, extending beyond formal language structure. In the realm of fake news, recognizing the significance of the pragmatic aspect is crucial. This involves analyzing how language operates in real-life situations to achieve specific effects. Consider the deceptive allure of a news headline such as Industry "Expert Reveals Shocking Secrets." Here, the pragmatic meaning is intricately tied to the context of readership expectations and the inherent desire for sensational revelations. In this instance, the word "expert" is strategically chosen to lend authority to the information, while "shocking secrets" cater to the reader's curiosity and appetite for sensationalism. The pragmatic effect is a headline that not only captures attention but also shapes the audience's perception of the information, creating an illusion of credibility and urgency. Pragmatics, therefore, plays a pivotal role in the strategic deployment of language within the context of fake news, allowing for the manipulation of readers' emotions, beliefs, and reactions.

References

Allcott, H., & Gentzkow, M. (2017). Social media and fake news in the 2016 election. *Journal of Economic Perspectives, 31*(2), 211–236.

Bakir, V., & McStay, A. (2018). Fake news and the economy of emotions: Problems, causes, solutions. *Digital Journalism, 6*(2), 154–175.

Barthes, R. (1970). *Mythologies*. Editions Du Seuil.

Barthes, R. (1972). *Mythologies*. Hill and Wang.

Biltoft, C. (2020). *Myth and misinformation, or the historian as semioclast*. https://www.graduateinstitute.ch/communications/news/myth-and-misinformation-or-historian-semioclast

Brewer, R. L. (2020). Semantics vs. syntax vs. pragmatics (grammar rules). *Writer's Digest*. https://www.writersdigest.com/write-better-fiction/semantics-vs-syntax-vs-pragmatics-grammar-rules

Chandler, D. (1994). *Semiotics for beginners*. https://www.cs.princeton.edu/~chazelle/courses/BIB/semio2.htm

Chaykowski, K. (2018). The disturbing focus of Juul's early marketing campaigns. *Forbes*. https://www.forbes.com/sites/kathleenchaykowski/2018/11/16/the-disturbing-focus-of-juuls-early-marketing-campaigns/?sh=46fe8a6914f9

de Saussure, F. (1916/1959). *Course in general linguistics* (C. Bally & A. Sechehaye, Eds.; W. Baskin, Trans.). The Philosophical Library.

Franco, A. (2017) Political polarization, the problem of fake news, and the responsibility of the user. *Communication & Society, 30*(1), 173–186.

Gorman, J., & Gorman, J. (2016). *Scientific myths that are too good to die*. Yale University Press.

Greimas, A. J. (1987). *Essays. Selections* (P. J. Perron & F. H. Collins, Trans.). University of Minnesota Press.

Hébert, L., & Tabler, J. (2019). *An introduction to applied semiotics* (1st ed.). Routledge.

Kolbert, E. (2017). Why facts don't change our minds. *The New Yorker*.

Morris, C. W. (1938). *Foundations of the theory of signs*. University of Chicago Press.

Morris, C. W. (1946/1955). *Signs, language and behavior*. Prentice-Hall.

Morris, C. W. (1971). *Writings on the general theory of signs*. Mouton.

Mercier, H., & Sperber, D. (2017). *The enigma of reason*. Harvard University Press.

Peirce, C. S. (1877). *The fixation of belief*. Popular Science Monthly, *12*(Nov 1877–Apr 1878).

Peirce, C. S. (1931). *The collected papers of Charles Sanders Peirce, Vol. I: The principles of philosophy (CP 1)* (C. Hartshorne & P. Weiss, Eds.). Harvard University Press.

Peirce, C. S. (1932). *The collected papers of Charles Sanders Peirce, Volumes I and II: Principles of philosophy and elements of logic (CP 1 and 2)* (C. Hartshorne & P. Weiss, Eds.). Harvard University Press.
Peirce, C. S. (1958). *The collected papers of Charles Sanders Peirce (Vols. 1–8, A. W. Burks, Ed.)*. Harvard University Press.
Reuters Institute. (2017). *Digital news report 2017: Tracking the future of news*. Oxford University.
Schwartz, J. (2018). Trump opens rift in press corps as he disses CNN as 'fake' and Fox News as 'real'. *Politico.* https://www.politico.com/story/2018/07/13/trump-media-cnn-fox-fake-news-719279

CHAPTER 4

Fake News Discourse: Semiotic Analyses Examples

Abstract This chapter aims to explore the application of semiotic frameworks in unraveling deceptive narratives. It commences with a sharp analysis of deepfakes in an Indian election campaign through Roland Barthes's lens, revealing the strategic manipulation of signs and symbols in political landscapes. Throughout the chapter, the meticulous deconstruction of semiotic codes goes beyond merely identifying misinformation, aspiring to empower readers with a profound understanding of the intricate layers underpinning the dissemination of deceptive information. The chapter concludes with an analysis of Charles William Morris's semiotic dimensions within fabricated stories, offering comprehensive insights into the intricate interplay of semiotic elements in narrative construction. perception.

Keywords Semiotic frameworks · Strategic manipulation · Misinformation · Semiotic codes · Cultural landscape · Political landscape

T. Iskanderova, *Unveiling Semiotic Codes of Fake News and Misinformation*, https://doi.org/10.1007/978-3-031-53751-6_4

INTRODUCTION

This chapter presents a rigorous examination centered on the application of semiotic frameworks to deceptive narratives. The narrative entails an analytical exploration of communication theories and their consequential impact on constructing misleading stories.

The chapter is initiated with analyses of deepfakes within an Indian election campaign, according to Roland Barthes. The context of deepfakes within this political landscape becomes a pivotal subject of exploration. Barthes's meticulous analysis systematically dissects the intricate web of signs and symbols, emphasizing their utilization in deceptive narratives. This examination serves as an illuminating paradigm, elucidating the multifaceted nature of semiotic codes and their strategic manipulation for political ends.

Throughout each section, the chapters meticulously deconstruct semiotic codes' role in configuring deceptive narratives. The objective extends beyond the mere identification of misinformation, seeking to empower readers with a profound and nuanced comprehension of the intricate layers that underpin the dissemination of deceptive information.

An analysis of Charles William Morris's semiotic dimensions within fabricated stories concludes the exploration, furnishing a comprehensive understanding of the intricate interplay of semiotic elements in narrative construction. Morris's insights provide valuable perspectives on how these elements contribute to the nuanced crafting of narratives, subsequently influencing the perception and interpretation of information.

As the narrative progresses through these analytical segments, the overarching objective is to decode the complex interplay of signs and symbols. Consequently, readers are endowed with a profound insight into the semiotic intricacies that delineate the landscape of fake news. The analytical journey through these chapters assumes the character of a quest for truth within the intricate dynamics of communication, wherein the decoding of semiotic elements emerges as an imperative skill in navigating the evolving landscape of information.

Application of Roland Barthes's Semiotic Theory: Deepfakes in an Indian Election Campaign

In this section, a detailed exploration of the practical application of Roland Barthes's semiotic theory is undertaken through a focused analysis of the use of deepfakes in an Indian election campaign. A specific instance of fake news spread using the semioclasm approach, particularly from the perspective of mythology, will be described. The example mentioned above is detailed in the publication "The First Use of Deepfakes in an Indian Election Campaign" (Chawla, 2020).

Deepfakes in an Indian Election Campaign: Background

On February 7, 2020, a day ahead of the Legislative Assembly elections in Delhi, a significant political twist unfolded when two videos surfaced, leaving a lasting impact on the electoral landscape. These videos featured Manoj Tiwari, the prominent leader of the Bharatiya Janata Party (BJP), strategically criticizing Arvind Kejriwal, the incumbent in the Delhi government. However, what made these videos particularly noteworthy was the utilization of cutting-edge technology—deep fake.

In the first video, Tiwari eloquently expressed his criticisms of Arvind Kejriwal in English, reaching out to a wider audience and making a direct appeal to the electorate to consider voting for the BJP. The twist came in the second video, where Tiwari seamlessly switched to Haryanvi, a Hindi dialect known to be spoken by a significant portion of the BJP's target voters. This bilingual approach aimed to establish a deeper connection with the local population, showcasing a nuanced understanding of linguistic diversity within the constituency.

The orchestration of this digital campaign was attributed to the collaboration between the BJP and The Ideaz Factory, a prominent political communications company. Their intent was clear: to harness the potential of deep fake technology to craft a "positive campaign." The videos, skillfully manipulated through this advanced technology, aimed to present a persuasive narrative that resonated with the electorate.

While many popular deepfake videos are complete face swaps, in the above-mentioned video, only the lip movements were changed to match the target audio. It is a subtle version of deepfake. "We used a 'lips-sync'

deepfake algorithm and trained it with speeches of Manoj Tiwari to trans-
late audio sounds into basic mouth shapes," says Sagar Vishnoi, The Ideaz
Factory's chief strategist (Chawla, 2020).

"The Haryanvi videos let us convincingly approach the target audience even if the candidate didn't speak the language of his voter," said
BJP's Bakshi (Paymaster). The response to those videos was encouraging.
According to the housewives' comments on the above-mentioned WhatsApp group, it was heartening for them to watch their leader speak their
language (Chawla, 2020).

Tiwari's fabricated video was used widely to dissuade the Haryanvi-
speaking migrant workers, the largest part of the Delhi population,
from voting for his political opponent. These deepfakes were distributed
across 5800 WhatsApp groups in the Delhi and NCR region, reaching
approximately 15 million people (Chawla, 2020).

Application of Semioclasm Approach (Mythology Point of View)

The semiotic analysis of the fabricated videos featuring Manoj Tiwari
in the context of an Indian election campaign draws upon Roland
Barthes's perspective, shedding light on the intricacies of sign systems
and their profound impact on shaping public perceptions. Taking a *semioclasm* (Barthes, 1970) approach, which involves revealing the constructed
nature of social norms and exposing ways in which they contribute
to manipulation, we aim to scrutinize the representations or myths
constructed in these videos. Through this lens, we endeavor to reveal
the hidden meanings and subtexts that play a pivotal role in influencing
and manipulating public opinion.

Analysis of Visual Elements

Denotation: From a denotational point of view, the videos present non-
coded iconic signs that form the visual language of the political narrative.
Manoj Tiwari, dressed in a gray suit and a white t-shirt, is strategically
positioned within an office setting, directly addressing the camera. The
backdrop consists of a green-colored wall, providing a distinct visual
context. Notably, a piece of saffron cloth is visibly placed behind Tiwari,
contributing to the overall visual composition.

Connotation: Analyzing the videos from a *connotational perspective*
reveals the nuanced, coded messages and signs strategically embedded in
the visual narrative. Manoj Tiwari is carefully portrayed as a professional

figure, a characterization crafted through meticulous choices in his attire and the calculated setting within an office.

The deliberate selection of colors in the visual composition, such as the saffron cloth, white t-shirt, and green wall, extends beyond mere aesthetics. These hues, mirroring the tricolors of the Indian flag, carry symbolic weight. Tiwari's juxtaposition with these colors is intended to symbolize not only his professionalism but also his alignment with core national values—patriotism, power, and an integral role within the collective identity of the country. The color scheme constructs a narrative that aims to evoke a sense of national pride, positioning Tiwari as a figure deeply connected to the ethos of the nation.

The green color of the wall holds connotations of new beginnings within Indian culture. This choice taps into cultural symbols associated with harvest, happiness, and optimism, contributing to an overarching narrative of promise and growth. It aligns with cultural narratives that resonate with themes of prosperity and positive transformation.

The utilization of a close-up camera shot in the videos introduces another layer to the connotational analysis. By framing Tiwari intimately, the visual narrative seeks to establish a personal connection between the political figure and each potential voter. This technique aims to create a sense of familiarity and direct engagement, fostering the illusion that Tiwari is speaking individually to every viewer. This connotational strategy enhances the perceived authenticity and relatability of the candidate, strengthening the emotional connection with the audience.

In unraveling the connotational intricacies of the visual elements, we find a semiotic narrative that transcends the surface, weaving together symbols and imagery to construct a compelling representation of Manoj Tiwari.

Analysis of the linguistic message: The linguistic *message* within the videos involves Tiwari criticizing his political opponent for unfulfilled promises. This verbal narrative, coupled with the strategic deployment of the Haryanvi dialect in the second video, adds a layer of cultural resonance to the communication strategy. By incorporating the dialect spoken by the target audience, Tiwari endeavors to create an illusion of profound personal connection, further reinforcing the myth that he not only comprehends but genuinely speaks the language of his constituents.

Concluding the above-mentioned in the video spots, Manoj Tiwary is represented as a highly professional and patriotic candidate, who does care about his voters and will bring a new direction to the political and social life of India in case of his successful election.

However, applying semioclastic scrutiny to these videos unveils the subtle manipulation at play. While the videos may seem like standard political outreach, the revelation that Tiwari is delivering a message in a dialect he doesn't speak exposes the semiotic illusion. The lip movements were altered using a "lips-sync" deepfake algorithm, emphasizing the disconnection between the perceived and actual communication. The analysis of the video through the lens of Roland Barthes's (1970) semiotic theory reveals how coded messages and signs can be used to convey a particular image of a political candidate and influence viewers' perceptions. As technology continues to advance, it is essential to remain vigilant and aware of the potential misuse of deepfake technology in politics and beyond.

The response to these deepfakes, particularly from the Haryanvi-speaking migrant workers, showcases the impact of manipulating signs. The fabricated videos, distributed widely on WhatsApp, aimed to dissuade this significant population from supporting Tiwari's political opponent (Chawla, 2020). The success of this strategy, as evidenced by the encouraging comments within WhatsApp groups, highlights the potency of semiotic manipulation in shaping perceptions.

In examining this case through the lens of Roland Barthes's semiotic theory, it becomes evident how coded messages, visual elements, and linguistic choices can construct a particular image of a political candidate, influencing the viewers' perceptions. As technology advances, the potential misuse of deepfake technology raises ethical concerns, emphasizing the need for vigilance in safeguarding the integrity of political discourse and public opinion.

Application of Algirdas Julien Greimas and Joseph Courtés Semiotic Theory: "The Ghost of Kyiv" Fake News

In this section, we explore the practical application of Algirdas Julien Greimas and Josef Courtés' semiotic theory of veridictory square through a focused analysis of the "Ghost of Kyiv" fake news story.

"The Ghost of Kyiv" Fake News Story: Background

The fake news story claimed that a MiG-29 pilot nicknamed the "Ghost of Kyiv" shot down six Russian planes during the initial invasion. However, the identity of the pilot was never confirmed, and multiple sources suggest that the story was likely a part of an "information war" to counter the Russian invasion. Former Ukrainian president Petro Poroshenko even tweeted a photo falsely claiming it to be the "Ghost of Kyiv." Ukraine's Air Force Command later admitted that the "Ghost of Kyiv" was a mythical character created by Ukrainians to boost morale (Eisele, 2022).

As it was found later, the video shorts of the "Ghost of Kyiv" were a computer-generated video of a dogfight between a Ukrainian pilot called the "Ghost of Kyiv" and a Russian plane that was uploaded on *YouTube* using a video game in 2013. The video was shared by the official Twitter account of the Armed Forces of Ukraine but was later debunked by *Snopes* (a social media fact-checking website), which proved the video was miscaptioned.

Application Algirdas Julien Greimas and Joseph Courtés Theory of Veridictory Square

Applying the Greimas and Courtés theory of the veridictory square to analyze the fake news story surrounding the "Ghost of Kyiv" involves a detailed semiotic examination using various markers: (1) the observing subject (S1, S2, etc.), (2) the object being observed (O1, O2, etc.), (3) the characteristic of the object being observed (C1, C2, etc.), (4) the marker(s) for seeming and being (M1, M2), (5) the four terms: being and seeming and their negations, not-being, and not-seeming. (6) the four metaterms that define the four veridictory categories, (7) the object's position on the square, and (8) time (T).

1. *The observing subject (S)*: Various sources, including the Security Service of Ukraine, Ukrainian soldiers and civilians, and media outlets, have reported on The Ghost of Kyiv.
2. *The object being observed (O)*: The "Ghost of Kyiv", a mythical MiG-29 Fulcrum flying ace credited with shooting down six Russian planes over Kyiv during the Kyiv offensive on February 24, 2022.

3. *The characteristic of the object being observed (C)*: The "Ghost of Kyiv" is a myth credited as a morale booster for Ukrainians and as a narrative for Ukraine's success during the invasion.

4. *The marker(s) for seeming and being (M1, M2)*: Seeming refers to how something appears or is perceived while being refers to what something actually is. The Ghost of Kyiv seemed to be a real person who shot down six Russian planes, but in reality, he did not exist.

5. *The four terms*:

   a. *Being*:
      - The fake news story claimed that the "Ghost of Kyiv" shot down six Russian planes during the initial invasion.
      - Former Ukrainian president Petro Poroshenko even tweeted a photo falsely claiming it to be the "Ghost of Kyiv."
      - The video shorts of the "Ghost of Kyiv" were a computer-generated video of a dogfight between a Ukrainian pilot called the "Ghost of Kyiv" and a Russian plane that was uploaded on YouTube using a video game in 2013.

   b. *Seeming*:
      - The identity of the pilot was never confirmed.
      - Multiple sources suggest that the story was likely part of an "information war" to counter the Russian invasion.
      - The "Ghost of Kyiv" was a mythical character created by Ukrainians to boost morale.
      - The video was shared by the official Twitter account of the Armed Forces of Ukraine but was later debunked by Snopes, which proved the video was miscaptioned.

   c. *Not-Being*:
      - The "Ghost of Kyiv" did not actually shoot down six Russian planes.
      - The "Ghost of Kyiv" was not a real person.

   d. *Not-Seeming*:
      - The story was not true and was likely part of an "information war" to counter the Russian invasion.
      - The video was not authentic and was uploaded on YouTube using a video game in 2013.
      - The photo tweeted by Poroshenko was not of the Ghost of Kyiv.

6. *The four metaterms*:

- *True or truth (B + S)*: The "Ghost of Kyiv" is not a real person but a myth created for moral and narrative purposes.
- *Illusory or lie (NB + S)*: The belief in the "Ghost of Kyiv" as a real person who shot down six Russian planes is a falsehood.
- *False or falsehood (NB + NS)*: The "Ghost of Kyiv" did not exist, so the claim that he shot down six Russian planes is a falsehood.
- *Secret or dissimulation (B + NS)*: The creation and spread of the "Ghost of Kyiv" myth was intentionally fabricated to deceive and manipulate people's perceptions of the conflict.

7. *The object's position on the square*: The object's position on the veridictory square is in the quadrant of lie (4), where there is a seeming appearance of truth, but in reality, it is a fabrication meant to deceive people.
8. *Time*: The belief in The "Ghost of Kyiv" as a real person who shot down six Russian planes was prevalent during and shortly after the Kyiv offensive. However, two months later, the Ukrainian Air Force acknowledged the myth's falsehood.

The analysis of the fake news story about the "Ghost of Kyiv" using the Greimas and Courtés semiotic theory of veridictory square reveals that the story was a fabricated myth created for morale and narrative purposes during the Russian invasion. The story appeared to be true or seemed to be true, but in reality, it was a falsehood meant to deceive people.

The object's position on the veridictory square is in the quadrant of Lie (4), where there is a seeming appearance of truth, but in reality, it is a fabrication intended to manipulate people's perceptions of the conflict. The belief in the myth was prevalent during and shortly after the Kyiv offensive, but it was later debunked, and the Ukrainian Air Force acknowledged its falsehood two months later. This example highlights the importance of fact-checking and verifying sources before spreading information, particularly during times of conflict or crisis.

Application of Charles Saunders Peirce's Semiotic Theory: "Comet Ping Pong" Fake News; "Supposed Offshore Account of Emmanuel Macron" Fake News

In this section, we explore the practical application of Charles Peirce's semiotic theory, closely examining two distinct incidents. These occurrences serve as compelling examples, illustrating the significant influence of belief fixation methods and the principles of association in shaping our perception of reality.

In the exploration of Charles Saunders Peirce's belief fixation methods and their practical application, a vivid example emerges through the unsettling incident known as "Pizzagate." This incident, which unfolded at Comet Ping Pong, a pizza shop in northwest Washington, D.C., serves as a stark illustration of how the above-mentioned methods, as outlined by Peirce, can have profound real-world implications.

In delving into Charles Peirce's three principles of association and their practical application, a compelling instance unfolds through the examination of the disconcerting incident known as the "Supposed Offshore Account of Emmanuel Macron." This example, sourced from François Allard Huver's publication "Between Disinformation Tactics and Deciphering Strategies: Towards a Semio-political Analysis of 'Fake News' and 'Alternative Facts'" (2019), provides a valuable lens to understand how Peirce's principles of association come into play in the dissemination of false information.

"Comet Ping Pong" Fake News: Background

On a Sunday in December 2016, a disturbing incident occurred at Comet Ping Pong, a pizza shop in northwest Washington D.C.. In the middle of a busy day in a peaceful shopping district filled with families, a man entered the shop with a rifle and began shooting. Fortunately, no one was harmed, and the suspect was apprehended. The shocking motive behind this crime is traced back to false tweets circulating online about Comet Ping Pong being involved in a baseless pedophile sex ring, implicating Democratic presidential candidate Hillary Clinton and members of her campaign (Stelter, 2016).

The perpetrator, 28-year-old Edgar M. Welch from Salisbury, N.C., had read online allegations that the pizza restaurant was harboring young children as part of a child abuse ring led by Clinton. Concerned by the misinformation, Welch drove about six hours to investigate the situation himself. Upon arriving, he fired shots from an AR-15 rifle but was swiftly arrested. The police found a rifle and a handgun in the restaurant, with no injuries reported (Stelter, 2016).

The origin of the misinformation can be traced back to the hacking of John Podesta's email account, whose leaked emails, published by WikiLeaks, led to speculations on online platforms like 4Chan. That idea jumped to other social media services such as Twitter and Reddit, where it gained momentum on the page *The_Donald* (pages of another presidential candidate from the Republican party Donald Trump). A new Reddit discussion thread called "Pizzagate" quickly attracted 20,000 subscribers (Borchers, 2016).

The pizza shop operators faced threats from right-wing activists who believed in the baseless reports. The trigger for this escalation was linked to the FBI's announcement on October 28 about resuming the investigation into Hillary Clinton's use of private email during her tenure as Secretary of State. False tweets about a pedophile sex ring surfaced, and posts on anonymous bulletin board sites intensified, focusing on Comet Ping Pong. Even after the presidential election, the hashtag #pizzagate persisted.

Reports suggested CIA findings of cyber-attacks on Democratic Party officials' emails, indicating Russian intervention aimed at influencing the election. As belief in the "Pizzagate" conspiracy grew, so did threats to the pizza shop and surrounding businesses. Despite social media bans on related posts, the threats continued, culminating in a 28-year-old man from North Carolina showing up at the shop with a rifle, claiming to conduct his own "investigation." In a New York Times interview after his capture, he expressed a misguided intent to rescue children he believed were trapped in the shop (Borchers, 2016).

Application of Charles Saunders Peirce's Belief Fixation Methods

Examining the "Pizzagate" incident through Peirce's (1877) exploration of belief fixation methods reveals a disturbing interplay of these methods, leading to real-world consequences.

1. *Method of tenacity*: The "Pizzagate" incident vividly illustrates *the* method of tenacity, where individuals like Edgar M. Welch clung

unwaveringly to false beliefs despite contradictory evidence. The false tweets about Comet Ping Pong persisted, leading Welch to take drastic actions, such as driving for hours to the pizza shop to investigate, demonstrating an immediate and decisive response characteristic of the tenacity method. Online discourse, especially on platforms like Twitter and Reddit, becomes a breeding ground for tenacity, with individuals resisting the complexity of the situation and clinging to their ideas even in the face of contrary information.

2. *Method of authority*: In the context of "Pizzagate," the influence of authoritative figures, including political figures like Hillary Clinton and President Trump, significantly impacted beliefs within the community. The involvement of the FBI in the narrative further underscores the authority's role in shaping public perception. Media outlets' interpretation of facts played a pivotal role in amplifying the false allegations, highlighting how the *method of authority* can lead to the widespread adoption of baseless beliefs, contributing to polarization within communities.

3. *A priori method*: The misinformation campaign surrounding "Pizzagate" exemplifies the A Priori Method, with confirmation bias evident in the selection and acceptance of information on platforms like Facebook. Users actively sought information that aligned with their existing beliefs, contributing to the formation of filter bubbles and echo chambers. The quick uptake of the false narrative on 4Chan and its subsequent spread on various social media platforms, including Twitter and Reddit, emphasizes how preconceived notions shape the information individuals are willing to accept as true. This method reinforces the reluctance to entertain conflicting opinions, contributing to the polarization of beliefs.

4. *Scientific method*: In contrast to the aforementioned methods, the scientific method emphasizes shared beliefs based on repeatable processes and external observations. The absence of such a method in the "Pizzagate" incident is evident in the lack of objective evidence supporting the claims. The Scientific Method involves reasoning and observation, which, if properly followed, should lead individuals to a shared conclusion based on empirical reality.

As we unravel the layers of belief fixation in the "Pizzagate" incident, it becomes evident how these methods contribute to the shaping of narratives, the polarization of communities, and, in extreme cases, the manifestation of real-world threats. Understanding these dynamics is essential for navigating the complex interplay between belief and behavior in the age of information.

"Supposed Offshore Account of Emmanuel Macron" Fake News: Background

The fabrication metamorphosed into an alternative fact, weaving a narrative around the purported offshore account of Emmanuel Macron. This misinformation surfaced on the internet mere hours before the conclusion of the official 2017 French presidential election campaign.

Within the same batch of documents, a statement allegedly from the First Caribbean International Bank bore the signature of the candidate, seemingly confirming the existence of a concealed offshore account. However, the facade quickly unraveled. A few hours later, both French news sites and unidentified users on 4chan exposed the glaring flaws in the fabrication. A meticulous examination by a graphic designer, who opened the PDF document on Adobe Illustrator, revealed a critical oversight by the forger—failure to "merge" the distinct layers of the original forged document. The concocted narrative entwined actual names sourced from other leaked documents with fabricated signatures and information. The intention behind disseminating these fraudulent documents was to sow confusion by insinuating that these fabrications held the status of exposed secrets (Allard-Huver, 2019).

Application of Charles Peirce's Three Principles of Association

Based on Peirce's (1932) three principles of association, the alternative fact about Emmanuel Macron's supposed offshore account is a clear example of how false information can spread quickly and widely in the digital age.

1. The *principle of resemblance (sense of similar qualities)* suggests that we tend to associate things that share similar characteristics. In this case, the alternative fact about Macron's offshore account gained traction because it was consistent with a broader narrative about political corruption and secret financial dealings. The story may have seemed plausible to some because it fits within a larger framework of mistrust toward politicians and the global elite.

2. The *principle of contiguity (proximity in time or space)* is another principle of association that can help explain why the alternative fact about Macron's offshore account gained traction. The story broke just a few hours before the end of the official 2017 French presidential election campaign, which meant that it was likely to attract attention from voters and the media. The timing of the release may have also made the story seem more credible, as people may have assumed that it was part of a last-minute attempt to sway the election.

3. Analyzing the false document through Peirce's third principle, the *principle of causality*, emphasizes the association of ideas leading to a sense of learning. The fake document claims to provide a representation of a fact, suggesting that through contemplation, one can acquire additional knowledge about the subject.

In this case, the alternative fact about Macron's offshore account may have resonated with people because it tapped into pre-existing beliefs about the corrupt nature of politics and the need for transparency in public life. According to the veridictory square (Greimas, 1987), we find ourselves in a situation where lies, non-being, and appearing are at the heart of the public sphere and within the framework of a political system that favors the existence of these lies. Hannah Arendt distinguishes two forms of lies: traditional lies linked to secrets and data that had never been made public, and modern lies that deal with things that are by no means secrets.

However, if most of the forged documents followed a clear political goal, some of them had a "lighter" purpose and were created as jokes. For instance, in a fake email, the general secretary of En Marche states his love for "Yaoi," "progressive metal," and confesses that he watched the ten seasons of Doctor Who! Similarly, another email claims that Emmanuel Macron is going to impose the expression "chocolatine" instead of "pain au chocolat" in France. Of course, Emmanuel Macron's email account was noticeably a joke: "em_UltraBG.Macron@en-marche.net," with "BG" meaning "good-looking guy" in slang (Allard-Huver, 2019).

Since the leak, the platform released more than 21,000 "real" authentic emails from Emmanuel Macron's campaign team. Nonetheless, those who leaked the documents leaned on today's information consumption and social media uses to spread the idea that Macron was hiding the truth about his campaign. The exchange of tweets during the leaks is typical of the tendency to share information that is "crowd-curated" rather than curated by specialists like editors, and most of the links shared are not read by those who share them. This is typical of modern information consumption. People form an opinion based on a summary or summary of summaries without making the effort to go deeper (Allard-Huver, 2019).

The example of fake news about Emmanuel Macron's supposed offshore account demonstrates how false information can spread quickly and widely in the digital age. Based on Charles Peirce's three principles of association, the alternative fact gained traction because it was consistent with a broader narrative about political corruption and secret financial dealings, broke just before the end of the French presidential election campaign and tapped into pre-existing beliefs about the need for transparency in public life. The way this false information was spread highlights the tendency for people to form opinions based on summaries without making an effort to go deeper, a typical characteristic of modern information consumption.

APPLICATION OF CHARLES WILLIAM MORRIS'S SEMIOTIC THEORY: "POPE SLAPS TRUMP" FAKE NEWS VIDEO AND "OCASIO-CORTEZ PROPOSES NATIONWIDE MOTORCYCLE BAN" FAKE NEWS

In this section, we apply Charles William Morris's semiotic theory to practical scenarios, dissecting two instances of fake news through specific semiotic dimensions. Our goal is to shed light on how Morris's framework, which includes sign vehicle, designatum, interpretant, and interpreter as its four elements of semiosis, reveals intentional strategies used in crafting and spreading deceptive narratives.

In demonstrating the four elements of semiosis practical application, we will analyze a fake video depicting Pope Francis supposedly slapping Donald Trump's hand. By dissecting these semiotic dimensions, we aim to reveal the intentional strategies employed in the creation and dissemination of deceptive narratives within the realm of fake news.

Examining the fake news, "Ocasio-Cortez Proposed Nationwide Motorcycle Ban," through Charles William Morris's syntax, semantic and pragmatic semiotic dimensions expose calculated strategies. The clickbait title and false content strategically generate controversy on social media, emphasizing the critical importance of fact-checking and discernment in navigating misinformation.

"Pope Slaps Trump" Fake News Video: Background

A fake video circulating on social media appears to show Pope Francis slapping Donald Trump's hand during their meeting at Vatican City in 2017. Before their meeting at Vatican City, Pope Francis and Donald Trump had been in a dispute, during which Francis had criticized Trump's comments about migrants as being against Christian values.

However, the video is fake and was created and aired as part of a comedic skit by "Jimmy Kimmel Live." A spokesperson for CNN, whose logo appears in the fake video, confirmed that the clip was fabricated and was never broadcast by the network. The original footage shows Trump and the Pope posing for pictures, but it does not zoom in on their hands, and none of the footage shows the Pope slapping Trump's hand (Lee, 2022).

Application of Charles William Morris's Four Elements of Semiosis

Analyzing the fake video featuring Pope Francis and Donald Trump through Charles William Morris's semiotic lens provides insight into the deliberate strategies employed in its creation and dissemination:

1. *Sign Vehicles*: The fake video utilizes visual and auditory elements as *sign vehicles*, leveraging the format of a video to convey a misleading interaction between Pope Francis and Donald Trump. Crafted with precision, the video aims to resonate with the audience's emotions and biases, using humor to potentially mislead viewers. The sensational aspect of the video, portraying a slap, is strategically designed to capture attention and manipulate perceptions.
2. *Designatum*: In the realm of fake news, the *designatum* represents the distorted interpretation of reality that the sign aims to designate. In this case, the designatum is the fabricated slapping incident between Pope Francis and Donald Trump. The intentional distortion serves to evoke emotional responses, such as surprise or amusement, from the audience. By critically analyzing the designatum, one can uncover the underlying motive of the content

creators, who may seek to exploit the audience's emotional reactions for entertainment or other purposes.

3. *Interpretant*: The *interpretant* in this fake news context encompasses the emotional responses elicited from viewers upon perceiving the sign. The comedic nature of the fake video aims to evoke laughter or amusement as the interpretant. This deliberate cultivation of emotional reactions serves as a tool for the creators to entertain the audience. Understanding the interpretant sheds light on how emotional triggers are strategically harnessed to shape perceptions and influence the audience's response to the misinformation presented.

4. *Interpreter*: The *interpreter*, in the context of the fake video, represents individuals who may belong to specific political or ideological groups. While the video may not have a clear political agenda, it can resonate with those who enjoy humor or satire at the expense of political figures. The targeted audience likely includes individuals who appreciate comedic content and may not critically assess the authenticity of the video. The interpreter's existing beliefs and values align with the comedic narrative, reinforcing their perspective without necessarily promoting a specific political agenda.

This fake video employs semiotic dimensions to create a humorous but misleading narrative. Understanding the intricacies of sign vehicles, designatum, interpretant, and interpreter provides a comprehensive view of the intentional strategies used in crafting and disseminating such deceptive content.

"Ocasio-Cortez Proposed Nationwide Motorcycle Ban" Fake News: Background

In June 2019, a sensational article circulated on Facebook claiming that Junior Congresswoman Alexandria Ocasio-Cortez proposed a nationwide ban on motorcycles as part of her "Green New Deal" initiative. The post featured an image of Alexandria Ocasio-Cortez during an interview, accompanied by the headline "Ocasio-Cortez Proposed Nationwide Motorcycle Ban."

At first glance, the news could raise concerns, considering Alexandria Ocasio-Cortez's focus on environmental change and cleaner energy.

However, closer research revealed that it was another instance of fake news designed to attract attention with its clickbait title.

Further investigation, including a Google search with the title "Alexandria Ocasio-Cortez bans Motorcycles," led to numerous articles debunking the claim. Fact-checking websites, such as *Snopes*, categorically dismissed the news as false (Palma, 2019). The origin of this misinformation was traced back to a website called *Taters gonna taste*, dated April 6, 2019. Given Alexandria Ocasio-Cortez's status as the youngest woman in Congress, she often becomes a target for clickbait and hoaxes circulating on the internet (Fallisgunnington, 2016).

Taters gonna taste is identified as part of a network of junk news sites that spread political misinformation under the guise of satire. The ease of sharing on platforms like *Facebook* contributed to the virality of this article, despite its inaccuracies. The deceptive nature of such articles thrives because people often don't delve beyond the headlines.

While the fake news suggested a potential ban on motorcycles, the reality is that motorcycles, despite potential environmental concerns, are deeply ingrained in society. Arguments for banning motorcycles exist, citing reasons such as accidents, environmental impact, and noise. However, it remains highly improbable due to their significant contribution to the US economy and the enjoyment they bring to people. Additionally, no serious attempts have been made to ban motorcycles as they serve a societal purpose.

The *Taters Gonna Tate* website falsely reported on April 6, 2019, that Alexandria Ocasio-Cortez intended to draft legislation for a nationwide motorcycle ban. The fabricated story included statistics on accidents and injuries, relaxed traffic rules, and tolls for bikers. A veiled jab at a core demographic of President Trump's supporters added a sensational touch to the false narrative.

Application of Charles William Morris's Syntax, Semantic, and Pragmatic Dimensions

Continuing with the exploration of Morris's (1938) semiotic analysis, it becomes evident that each dimension, syntax, semantics, and pragmatics, contributes uniquely to the manipulation of information in this fake news scenario.

1. *Syntax*: In the context of *syntax*, the deliberate arrangement of words and phrases within the fake news structure is a calculated effort to create a striking impact. The clickbait title, with its concise and attention-grabbing language, serves as a powerful syntactic tool, orchestrating the reader's initial perception of the news.

2. *Semantics*: Moving to semantics, the intricacies of meaning woven into the narrative play a pivotal role in shaping public opinion. By associating the proposed motorcycle ban with Alexandria Ocasio-Cortez's "Green New Deal," the news strategically exploits semantic connections to cast a negative light on her environmental proposals. This intentional semantic distortion not only undermines her policy initiatives but also aims to tarnish her credibility in the eyes of the audience.

3. *Pragmatics*: In the realm of pragmatics, the news transcends the mere transmission of information, delving into the intended actions and reactions it seeks to elicit. The primary goal is to generate controversy, potentially targeting specific political groups or older generations. By exploiting existing controversies surrounding Alexandria Ocasio-Cortez's policies, the fake news seeks to leverage the divisive nature of these discussions. Furthermore, it takes advantage of the ease of sharing on social media platforms, where sensational content can quickly gain traction.

From a wider perspective, the examination underscores the crucial role of fact-checking and the verification of information sources. It illuminates the susceptibility of social media to the spread of misinformation, emphasizing the imperative for individuals to employ discernment and critical thinking while engaging with news content.

References

Allard-Huver, F. (2019). Between disinformation tactics and deciphering strategies: Towards a semio-political analysis of "fake news" and "alternative facts." *Semiotica*, 1–17.

Barthes, R. (1970). *Mythologies*. Editions Du Seuil.

Borchers, C. (2016, December 5). A harsh truth about fake news: Some people are super gullible. *The Washington Post*. https://www.washingtonpost.com/news/the-fix/wp/2016/11/22/a-harsh-truth-about-fake-news-some-peo ple-are-super-gullible/

Chawla, S. (2020). The first use of deepfakes in an Indian election campaign. *Journal of Political Marketing, 19*(2), 204–212.

Eisele, I. (2022). Fact check: Ukraine's 'Ghost of Kyiv' fighter pilot. *DW News.* Retrieved January 16, 2023, from https://www.dw.com/en/fact-check-ukr aines-ghost-of-kyiv-fighter-pilot/a-60951825

Fallisgunnington. (2016, April 6). Ocasio-Cortez Proposes Nationwide Motorcycle Ban. In *ALLODS.* https://tatersgonnatate.com/nobikes/?fbclid=IwA R25gkiUmSC2qKnItUnRyE8ke2C4osE8OyCQ-Mpb35dwJQ9NivNQQch 3XSk

Greimas, A. J. (1987). *Essays. Selections.* (P. J. Perron & F. H. Collins, Trans.). University of Minnesota Press.

Lee, M. (2022, September 19). Fact check: Fact check: Pope Francis Did NOT Slap Donald Trump's hand—It's a clip from a late-night TV show. *Lead Stories.* https://leadstories.com/hoax-alert/2022/09/fact-check-pope-fra ncis-did-not-slap-donald-trumps-hand-it-is-a-clip-from-a-late-night-tv-show. html

Morris, C. (1938). *Foundations of the theory of signs.* University of Chicago Press.

Palma, B. (2019, April 8). Did Alexandria Ocasio-Cortez Propose a Nationwide Motorcycle Ban? In *Snopes.* https://www.snopes.com/fact-check/aoc-motorc ycle-ban/

Peirce, C. S. (1877). The fixation of belief. *Popular Science Monthly, 12*(Nov 1877–Apr 1878).

Peirce, C. S. (1932). *The collected papers of Charles Sanders Peirce, Volumes I and II: Principles of philosophy and elements of logic (CP 1 and 2)* (C. Hartshorne & P. Weiss, Eds.). Harvard University Press.

Stelter, B. (2016, December 6). Fake news, real violence: 'Pizzagate' and the consequences of an Internet echo chamber. *CNN Business.* https://money. cnn.com/2016/12/05/media/fake-news-real-violencepizzagate/index.html

CHAPTER 5

Analysis of Fake News Narratives: Exercises

Abstract The chapter aims to serve as a practical bridge between theory and application by providing hands-on exercises for readers to refine their skills in recognizing and deconstructing deceptive narratives. Covering various approaches, such as Roland Barthes's semiotic theory and analyses influenced by Charles William Morris, these exercises explore different aspects, offering a flexible toolkit to decode complex semiotic codes. Beyond theoretical comprehension, the goal is to deepen readers' understanding, cultivate awareness, and develop a critical eye when encountering misleading information. Actively engaging with these exercises not only refines analytical skills but also builds a practical toolkit applicable beyond the chapter's scope. This chapter encourages active participation in decoding deceptive narratives, aligning with the overarching objective of fostering media literacy and critical thinking in the face of misinformation.

Keywords Hands-on exercises · Critical thinking · Misinformation · Semiotic codes

© The Author(s), under exclusive license to Springer Nature Switzerland AG 2024
T. Iskanderova, *Unveiling Semiotic Codes of Fake News and Misinformation*, https://doi.org/10.1007/978-3-031-53751-6_5

INTRODUCTION

This chapter offers a practical and interactive dimension, providing readers with hands-on exercises designed to refine their skills in recognizing and deconstructing deceptive narratives. This chapter serves as a crucial bridge between theoretical understanding and practical application, empowering readers to engage actively with the intricate subject matter.

The exercises provided in this chapter cover a variety of approaches, including applying Roland Barthes's semiotic theory and conducting detailed analyses influenced by Charles William Morris. Exploring the syntactic, semantic, and pragmatic aspects of these theories equips readers with a flexible set of tools to unravel the complex semiotic codes found within misleading narratives.

The goal of these exercises is not only to deepen readers' comprehension of the theoretical frameworks explored earlier but also to cultivate a heightened awareness and critical eye when encountering misleading information.

By actively engaging with these exercises, readers will not only refine their analytical skills but also develop a practical toolkit that can be applied beyond the scope of this exploration. This chapter invites readers to become active participants in the process of decoding and demystifying deceptive narratives, reinforcing the overarching objective of fostering media literacy and critical thinking in the face of misinformation.

APPLICATION OF ROLAND BARTHES'S
SEMIOTIC THEORY TO FAKE NEWS

Step I. Study a piece of fake news carefully (from print media, TV, internet, etc.). Identify between three and five significant signs to be decoded: For example, a claim is circulating on a social network within Central European social groups, stating that "COVID-19 Vaccine Causes Infertility In Women." The accompanying image in this fake news depicts a woman receiving a COVID-19 vaccine.

Signs to be decoded:

1. Image of a woman getting vaccinated
2. Headline of the article
3. Quotes from unidentified sources (from "doctors" or "medical professionals")

Step II. Perform analysis:

1. *Develop an introductory paragraph by describing the peace of news from a denotational point of view (non-coded messages):* The visual content shows a woman with blonde hair in a white summer dress receiving the COVID-19 vaccine. The title (the linguistic message) "COVID-19 Vaccine Causes Infertility In Women" explicitly asserts a direct causal link between the COVID-19 vaccine and female infertility. The reliable sources of the information remain unidentified.

   From a denotational perspective, these visual elements serve as clear representations without delving into additional layers of implied meaning. The focus remains on the surface-level information, showcasing a woman undergoing the vaccination procedure, without necessarily implying any specific attributes or connotations beyond the act itself.

2. *Develop a body section by describing the fake news from the connotational point of view (pre-planned or coded messages of the piece of news):*

   (a) *Image of a woman getting vaccinated (visual content):* The portrayal of a woman with blonde hair in a white summer dress receiving the COVID-19 vaccine adds connotational layers, invoking notions of vulnerability and relatability. In the Central European context, the color white carries symbolic associations with innocence and purity. The choice of a white summer dress in this depiction may subtly introduce connotations of the woman being an innocent victim of vaccination. This symbolic use of color amplifies the emotional impact of the image, potentially framing the act of vaccination as a threat to the perceived purity and innocence of the individual. The incorporation of cultural symbols enhances the connotational richness of the visual narrative, further shaping the audience's emotional response to the portrayed scenario.

   (b) *Headline of the article (linguistic message):* "COVID-19 Vaccine Causes Infertility In Women": The explicit assertion in the headline generates a signified message of fear and uncertainty regarding the safety of the COVID-19 vaccine. The combination of the alarming headline and the carefully constructed visual narrative serves to amplify the emotional impact, potentially fostering apprehension and skepticism among the Central European audience.

(c) *Quotes from doctors or medical professionals*: Furthermore, the use of quotes from unidentified sources, presented as doctors or medical professionals, introduces an element of authority to the claims made in the article. The signified message is the credibility attributed to these claims, despite the sources remaining undisclosed. This strategic use of unidentified quotes enhances the perceived reliability of the information, creating an illusion of expertise and contributing to the overall persuasive effect on the audience.

(d) *Proposed ideology*: The ideology proposed by the fake news article is that the COVID-19 vaccine is not safe and can cause harm, particularly infertility in women. This overarching narrative, reinforced through both visual and textual elements, aims to instill a sense of doubt and caution surrounding the vaccination process, potentially discouraging individuals from receiving the COVID-19 vaccine. The image of a woman getting vaccinated suggests that getting the vaccine can be dangerous and poses a risk of infertility.

Step III. Develop a conclusion paragraph, summarize your three to five signs and ideology. Consider what ideology/myth is constructed by the news story: The fake news article employs a multi-faceted approach to construct a narrative that undermines the safety of the COVID-19 vaccine, particularly within Central European social groups. The image of a woman with blonde hair in a white summer dress receiving the vaccine introduces connotational layers, subtly suggesting vulnerability and potential victimhood. The explicit headline, "COVID-19 Vaccine Causes Infertility In Women," generates fear and uncertainty regarding the vaccine's safety. The carefully orchestrated signs foster doubt and hesitation, potentially dissuading vaccination based on unfounded claims. This ideological framework, bolstered by visual and textual elements, serves to instill doubt and hesitation, potentially deterring individuals from pursuing vaccination based on misinformation and unsubstantiated claims.

APPLICATION OF ALGIRDAS JULIEN GREIMAS AND JOSEPH COURTÉS SEMIOTIC THEORY TO FAKE NEWS

Step I. Identify the claim: For instance, a fabricated news article from a US online source alleges the arrest of a well-known politician on corruption charges. The purported claim, insinuating the arrest of a prominent Democrat politician, takes a dubious turn in its origin. Departing from journalistic norms, this piece of misinformation did not arise from credible sources. Instead, it infiltrated the public sphere, particularly gaining traction among the Republican audience during the beginning of the presidential election campaign through widely used social networks.

Step II. Perform analysis:

A. *Develop an introductory paragraph by identifying the observing subject (S), the object being observed (O) and the characteristic of the object being observed (C)*:

1. *The observing subject (S)*: The individuals or entities actively engaged in observing and disseminating the news claims are multifaceted. This includes the online audience exposed to the fake news article, the social networks facilitating its circulation, and potentially those orchestrating the intentional spread of misinformation. Understanding the diverse perspectives and motivations within this observing subject is crucial for unraveling the impact and intent behind the dissemination of the fabricated claim.

2. *The object being observed (O)*: The central focus of attention is the news claim itself—the assertion that a prominent Democrat politician has been arrested for corruption charges. This news article, despite being unfounded, has become the focal point of discussion, sharing, and potential belief within the online community. Analyzing the nuances of how this object is perceived and interpreted by different segments of the audience is pivotal for a comprehensive assessment.

3. *The characteristic of the object being observed (C)*: The characteristic of the observed object lies in its deceptive nature and departure from journalistic integrity. This misinformation, not rooted in credible sources, introduces doubt about the accuracy

of the information presented. The characteristic of being politically charged, specifically targeting a Democrat politician, adds a layer of complexity and potential bias to the misinformation.

B. *Develop the second paragraph by identifying and describing the markers for seeming and being (M1, M2) and the four terms (Being, Seeming, Not-being, Not-seeming):*

1. The *marker(s) for seeming and being (M1, M2)*:
   - *M1 (marker for seeming)*: The deceptive nature of the news article is underscored by several markers. Anonymous sourcing and the absence of concrete evidence within the article contribute to the seeming appearance that the information may not be grounded in reality. Additionally, the use of sensationalized language further casts doubt on the credibility of the claim.
   - *M2 (marker for being)*: Conversely, the absence of official confirmation or tangible evidence serves as a significant marker for being. The lack of substantiated facts contributes to the skepticism surrounding the claim's authenticity. The news article lacks the necessary markers that would affirm the truthfulness of the politician's alleged arrest.

2. *The Four Terms*:
   - *Being*: The news article boldly asserts that the politician, specifically a Democrat, has been arrested on corruption charges. However, the absence of verifiable evidence weakens the claim's standing as a definitive truth.
   - *Seeming*: The article suggests, through anonymous sourcing and sensational language, that the politician is guilty of corruption. This introduces an appearance/reality gap, casting doubt on the accuracy of the information.
   - *Not-being*: There is no official confirmation or concrete evidence supporting the claims made in the news article. The absence of substantiated facts challenges the existence of the asserted arrest.
   - *Not-seeming*: Despite the suggestive language and sensationalism, there is no substantive evidence to support the claim. The seeming appearance of guilt lacks a solid foundation, making it not-seeming in the absence of credible verification.

C. *Develop the third paragraph by identifying and describing the four metaterms, the object's position on the veridictory square, and the element of time*:

1. *The Four Metaterms*:
   - *True or truth (B + S)*: The fabricated claim about the Democrat politician's arrest lacks veracity. While it may seem true on the surface, the absence of credible evidence and official confirmation positions it as a concocted narrative rather than an actual truth.
   - *Illusory or lie (NB + S)*: The illusion is crafted through deceptive markers within the article, such as anonymous sourcing and sensational language. This contributes to the illusion of a significant event (the arrest) without a foundation in reality.
   - *False or falsehood (NB + NS)*: The core assertion that the politician has been arrested is a falsehood, as it lacks both evidence and official confirmation. The claim is not substantiated by factual information, making it inherently false.
   - *Secret or dissimulation (B + NS)*: The creation and spread of this misinformation fall into the category of dissimulation. The intentional fabrication is geared toward deceiving and manipulating public perception, making it a strategic act of spreading disinformation.

2. *The object's position on the veridictory square*: The object, in this case, the news claim, occupies a precarious position on the veridictory square. It resides in quadrant 4 of lie (NB + S), where there is a seeming appearance of truth due to deceptive markers, but in reality, it is a falsehood. The illusion created by the markers conceals the lack of substantiated facts, placing the claim in a deceptive category.

3. *Time*: The belief in the news claim was prevalent during the beginning of the presidential election campaign, capturing the attention of the online audience and gaining traction. The strategic release of this misinformation during a politically charged period adds a layer of significance to its potential impact on public opinion and electoral dynamics.

Step III. Develop the Conclusion Paragraph:
Summarize your analysis in a few sentences by describing the wider situation of a fake story: The analysis of this fake news article reveals a deliberate attempt to manipulate public perception, particularly during the sensitive period of the presidential election campaign. The fabricated claim, suggesting the arrest of a prominent Democrat politician, exposes the strategic use of deceptive markers such as anonymous sourcing and sensational language. While initially gaining traction, the lack of credible evidence and official confirmation undermines the claim's veracity. This instance underscores the broader challenge of combating misinformation, emphasizing the critical role of fact-checking and source verification, especially in the context of heightened political sensitivity.

APPLICATION OF CHARLES SAUNDERS PEIRCE'S TO FAKE NEWS

Application of Charles Saunders Peirce's Belief Fixation Methods

Step I. Identify the claim: For example, a claim circulating on a social network stating that a new miracle health supplement can cure various illnesses, is backed by testimonials from unknown sources.

Step II. Assess the evidence: The evidence supporting this claim includes testimonials posted on the social network, praising the miraculous effects of the health supplement. However, there is a lack of verifiable scientific studies or reputable sources validating these test results.

Step III. Describe the false information from Peirce's belief fixation methods point of view:

1. *Method of tenacity*: Some individuals might fixate on this health claim through the method of tenacity, holding onto the belief despite any conflicting information. This could be due to personal experiences or a desire for the miracle cure to be true, reinforcing the belief irrespective of factual evidence.

2. *Method of authority*: Users may also adopt the method of authority, relying on influencers or celebrities endorsing the health supplement without critically evaluating the evidence. The appeal to authority can lead to belief fixation, as individuals trust the credibility of those promoting the product.

3. *A priori method*: A priori beliefs, existing before any evidence, might contribute to the fixation on this health claim. Users with pre-existing notions about alternative medicine or distrust in traditional healthcare may be more prone to accepting the information without demanding rigorous proof.

4. *Scientific method*: The scientific method, based on empirical evidence and systematic investigation, would highlight the lack of rigorous studies supporting the health claim. Those employing the scientific method would likely question the validity of the testimonials and seek robust scientific evidence before accepting the miraculous properties of the health supplement.

Step IV: Develop the conclusion paragraph:

Summarize your analysis in a few sentences by describing the wider situation of the fake news: The analysis through Charles Peirce's belief fixation methods unveils the various ways individuals may be led to accept false claims about miracle health supplements on social networks. The method of tenacity, relying on personal beliefs, the method of authority, trusting endorsements without scrutiny, and a priori beliefs, pre-existing notions shaping acceptance, all contribute to belief fixation. In the context of social networks, where information spreads rapidly, these methods can lead to the widespread acceptance of health claims without proper scrutiny. The scientific method, with its emphasis on empirical evidence, stands out as a crucial tool to discern fact from fiction in the realm of health information circulating on social media platforms.

Application of Charles Saunders Peirce's Three Principles of Association

Step I. Identify the claim:

For example, the claim described in Chapter 4. The claim in question asserts a candidate for the presidency possesses an offshore account, a statement later proven to be false.

Step II. Assess the evidence: The evidence supporting this claim includes a document purported to provide proof of the candidate's offshore accounts. However, upon examination, the document is revealed to be fabricated.

Step III. Describe the false information from Peirce's three principles of association point of view:

1. *Principle of resemblance (Similar Qualities)*: The false claim gains traction by aligning with a broader narrative of political corruption and secret financial dealings. Its resonance lies in its similarity to pre-existing suspicions about the opaque nature of global politics, making it seem plausible to some.

2. *Principle of contiguity (Proximity in Time or Space)*: The story broke just a few hours before the end of the official 2017 French presidential election campaign, which meant that it was likely to attract attention from voters and the media. The timing enhances its credibility, as it is perceived as a last-minute attempt to sway the election, garnering interest from voters and the media.

3. *Principle of causality (Association of Ideas Leading to Learning)*: Examining the false document through Peirce's third principle reveals its intent to convey knowledge through contemplation. By tapping into pre-existing beliefs about political corruption and the demand for transparency, the fabricated claim creates a sense of learning, further embedding it in the audience's perceptions.

Step IV: Develop the conclusion paragraph:

Summarize your analysis in a few sentences by describing the wider situation of the fake news: The analysis through Charles Peirce's three principles of association unveils the intricate web of psychological connections that facilitated the spread of the false claim about the candidate's alleged offshore account. The alignment with existing narratives of political corruption, coupled with strategic timing and the promise of gaining knowledge, propelled the misinformation's rapid dissemination. This case highlights the imperative for enhanced media literacy, emphasizing the discernment of psychological associations in navigating the digital information landscape.

APPLICATION OF CHARLES WILLIAM MORRIS'S SEMIOTIC THEORY TO FAKE NEWS

Application of Charles William Morris's Four Elements of Semiosis

Step I. Identify the claim: For example, a video that has been edited to make it look like a politician is saying something that they did not actually say. This video might be shared on social media platforms or other websites.

Step II. Identify the sign vehicle, designatum, interpretant and interpreter:

a. *Sign vehicle:* The sign vehicle of fake news can take many forms, including text, images, videos, and social media posts. These sign vehicles are carefully crafted to appeal to the emotions and biases of the intended audience, often with sensationalist headlines, provocative images, and misleading information. By analyzing the sign vehicles used in fake news, it becomes possible to identify the techniques and strategies used to manipulate and deceive the audience.

b. *Designatum:* The designatum of fake news refers to the kind of object or class of objects that the sign designates. In the case of fake news, the designatum is often a distorted or exaggerated version of reality, intended to create fear, outrage, or other emotional responses in the audience. By analyzing the designatum of fake news, it becomes possible to identify the underlying ideological or political agenda behind the content.

c. *Interpretant:* The interpretant of fake news refers to the disposition of an interpreter to initiate a response sequence as a result of perceiving the sign. In the case of fake news, the interpretant is often a strong emotional response, such as anger, fear, or disgust. These emotional responses can be exploited by the creators of fake news in order to manipulate and deceive the audience. By analyzing the interpretant of fake news, it becomes possible to understand the ways in which the audience is being manipulated.

d. *Interpreter:* The interpreter of the fake news story might be a member of a particular political or ideological group, whose beliefs and values are being reinforced by the content.

Step III. Perform Analysis:
Let's look at the above example:

a. *Sign vehicle:* The sign vehicle of this fake news example might be a video that has been edited to make it look like a politician is saying something that they did not actually say.

b. *Designatum:* The designatum of this fake news might be a false statement or claim that the politician is alleged to have made in the video. This could be something that is sensational or controversial, designed to elicit an emotional response from the audience.

c. *Interpretant*: The *interpretant* of this fake news might be outrage or anger from the audience in response to the false statement or claim made in the video. The emotional response of the audience can be exploited by the creators of the fake news to manipulate and deceive them.

d. *Interpreter*: The *interpreter* of this fake news might be people who are already aligned with a particular political party or ideology. The fake news might be designed to reinforce pre-existing beliefs or biases of the interpreter, thereby influencing their perception of the politician or the political party that the politician represents.

Step V. Develop the Conclusion Paragraph:
Summarize your analysis in a few sentences by describing the wider situation of the fake news: The manipulated video, acting as the sign vehicle, skillfully distorts reality, presenting a designatum of a false statement strategically crafted to evoke emotional responses, such as outrage or anger, from the audience. The interpretant becomes a tool for manipulation by creators seeking to deceive and exploit the emotions of the audience. The identified interpreter, aligned with a particular political group, further emphasizes the calculated nature of fake news, intending to reinforce existing beliefs and biases.

Application of Charles William Morris's Syntax, Semantic, and Pragmatic Dimensions

Step I. Identify the Claim: For example, a false blog article revolves around presenting information that may be entirely fabricated or taken out of context to create a misleading narrative. This could involve false statements, distorted facts, or sensationalized content designed to capture the reader's attention.

Step II. Identify Syntax, Semantic, and Pragmatic Dimensions:

a. *Syntax*: The false blog article employs a deliberate arrangement of words and phrases to construct a narrative that appears convincing. The choice of language is likely designed to be attention-grabbing, with sentence structures and writing styles carefully crafted to present misinformation. This syntactic manipulation aims to capture the reader's attention swiftly, potentially overshadowing critical evaluation.

b. *Semantics*: The false blog article introduces semantic distortion by presenting information that may be entirely fabricated or taken out of context. This intentional distortion plays a pivotal role in shaping public opinion. The article associates certain ideas or claims with emotionally charged language, aiming to evoke specific reactions from the readers. The semantics of the content are strategically designed to cast a negative light on a particular subject, potentially reinforcing existing biases and influencing perceptions.

c. *Pragmatics*: In the realm of pragmatics, the false blog article goes beyond the transmission of information. Its primary goal is likely to generate controversy and elicit emotional responses from the readers. This pragmatic objective may involve targeting a specific demographic or community, leveraging existing controversies or societal concerns. The article takes advantage of the ease of sharing on social media platforms, where sensational content can quickly gain traction, contributing to the pragmatic goal of reaching a wider audience. By exploiting a divisive nature, the article aims to influence discussions and opinions.

Step III. Perform Analyses:

a. *Syntax*: The deliberate arrangement of words and phrases serves to construct a narrative that appears convincing and attention-grabbing.

b. *Semantics*: Semantic distortion is evident as information is presented in a way that may be entirely fabricated or taken out of context. Emotionally charged language is strategically used to shape public opinion.

c. *Pragmatics*: Beyond information transmission, the article aims to generate controversy and elicit emotional responses. It likely targets specific demographics, leveraging social media for wider reach and contributing to the divisive nature of discussions.

Step IV. Develop the Conclusion Paragraph:

Summarize your analysis in a few sentences by describing the wider situation of the fake news: The false blog article strategically employs syntax, semantics, and pragmatics to create a misleading narrative. The deliberate syntactic structure captures attention, semantic distortion manipulates meaning to evoke emotional responses, and the pragmatic goal is to generate controversy and influence a specific audience.

INDEX

SPRINGER NATURE

GPSR Compliance

The European Union's (EU) General Product Safety Regulation (GPSR) is a set of rules that requires consumer products to be safe and our obligations to ensure this.

If you have any concerns about our products, you can contact us on ProductSafety@springernature.com

In case Publisher is established outside the EU, the EU authorized representative is:

Springer Nature Customer Service Center GmbH
Europaplatz 3
69115 Heidelberg, Germany

The manufacturer's authorised representative in the EU is Springer

Nature Customer Service Centre GmbH, Europaplatz 3, 69115 Heidelberg,

Germany. If you have any concerns regarding our products, please

contact ProductSafety@springernature.com

Printed and bound by CPI Group (UK) Ltd, Croydon, CR0 4YY

29/04/2026

02099525-0002